TROPICAL FISH

Douglas Gohm

Illustrations by David Carl Forbes;
photographs by Jane Burton,
Alan Cupit & Russ Kinne

TROPICAL
FISH

*Douglas
Gohm*

Hamlyn
London · New York · Sydney · Toronto

Originally published in 1952 by
C. Arthur Pearson Limited as
'Tropical Fish in the Home'.

Completely revised edition with
additional text and new illustrations
first published in 1970 by

THE HAMLYN PUBLISHING GROUP LIMITED
LONDON · NEW YORK · SYDNEY · TORONTO
Hamlyn House, Feltham, Middlesex, England

© The Hamlyn Publishing Group Limited 1970
Second Impression 1971
Third Impression 1972

ISBN 0 600 31616 5

PRINTED IN ITALY

Contents

List of colour

Jane Burton

Alan Cupit

Russ Kinne

Preface

Rarely is natural interaction in life observed very easily, yet our understanding, derived effectively and readily in both a practical and scientific sense, is one of the most rewarding aspects of keeping tropical fish. The environment contained in the relatively small world encompassed by the aquarium provides the means to study and experiment in a most convenient form, which can be limited or expanded according to financial resources, accommodation and personal inclinations.

Many aquarists are content to use their hobby as a means of home decoration, and enjoy the simple pleasure of watching the ever changing kaleidoscopic picture provided by the movement of exotically coloured fish. They are neither very interested in the art or scientific approach to the subject, but they are interested in keeping their aquariums trouble free.

Special attention has been given to the needs of the average and novice aquarist. The scientific information has been presented so that the text can be readily understood and care has also been taken in describing the coloration of the fish accurately, but some slight variation may occur due to the variability of specimens in respect of their colour.

Methods of breeding, where known, have been described, but occasionally spawnings will occur that are not quite to the expected. This is inevitable, as nature itself is continually experimenting and evolving.

It is, however, sincerely hoped that this book will give much pleasure and assistance to aquarists who are new to the hobby, and to those with a desire to experiment on their own behalf.

Aquaria

Importance of shape

A good aquarium is a planned fish community where the shape, size and layout are all important. It is true that some people have had good results with hit and miss methods, but they have been lucky. You can only be sure of success if you begin by considering the conditions under which the fish will live.

These conditions can be created by you, and in doing so you not only have to learn from nature, but improve upon nature to provide an ideal balanced world where different varieties of fish may be born, live together and thrive. This is not so simple as it may sound because nature has a way of striking a balance in the whole of her complicated structure; if she did not, the natural framework of animal and vegetable life would crumble. Therefore, unless we start with the *idea* of 'balance' foremost in our minds, it is likely that 'unbalanced' conditions in our aquariums may cause disastrous results.

A balanced aquarium, in a factual sense, is a myth. It implies that once an aquarium is set up it will look after itself—the plants giving off a balanced amount of oxygen to suit the needs of the fish, and the fish exhaling the necessary carbon dioxide required by the plants on a fair exchange basis. In fact, the oxygen content of water is more dependent on the surface area of water exposed to the atmosphere than it is on plant life. Under reasonable conditions, any oxygen deficiency is immediately made up from oxygen in the atmosphere passing into solution with the water.

Plants do help with the provision of oxygen when under the influence of strong light (see *photosynthesis*) and, if the oxygen so produced is excessive, it will pass off into the atmosphere. Bubbles of oxygen can often be seen rising to the surface from the plants.

Carbon dioxide, on the other hand, passes out of the water into the atmosphere at a much slower rate than oxygen. It is excessive carbon dioxide in the water that causes fish to rise to the surface 'gasping for air', not oxygen deficiency.

These facts show that a truly balanced aquarium is not possible to maintain in a technical sense.

However, the term is a good one, it suggests that the *aquarist* should maintain a balance by not overcrowding his fish; this will reduce the possibility of excessive carbon dioxide production. He should also ensure that the surface area of water is adequate, he should remove excessive excreta and debris, and he should not overfeed. In more general terms, maintaining balance means using common sense and knowledge to maintain a fish community in a 'balanced condition'.

The shape of the aquarium is the first consideration. It should not be too tall or narrow, as oxygen content, as previously stated, is more dependent upon surface area than on the actual volume of water.

An ideal size is 24 in. × 12 in. × 12 in., and this is an easy one to obtain if you prefer to buy a ready-made tank. I do not recommend the fancy shaped tanks many aquarists like to make for the odd corner or shelf because, although a tank of unusual size or shape may be decorative, it often has the limitations of a small surface area, and, apart from the right food and temperature, fish need plenty of room in which to live and become fully developed. If you restrict them to a confined space, or a tank with an inadequate surface area, you create an environment where they will be forced to adapt themselves by remaining small and stunted.

A tank 12 in. × 12 in. × 12 in. will contain one cubic foot of water with a surface area of one square foot. Indeed, the same quantity of water can be used in a tank 6 in. deep × 24 in. × 12 in., giving a surface area of two square feet. This larger tank will allow a greater number of fish to exist in comfort than in the one foot square tank, although both contain the same quantity of water.

To find how much water an aquarium will hold, use the following method of calculation:

$$\frac{Length\ in. \times Breadth\ in. \times Width\ in.}{1728} = \text{CAPACITY (cu. ft)}$$

The above formula gives the capacity in cubic feet and, as one cubic foot of water equals $6\frac{1}{4}$ gallons, you only have to multiply the product by $6\frac{1}{4}$ to find how many gallons the aquarium will hold.

One gallon of water weighs 10 lb.

One cubic foot of water weighs $62\frac{1}{2}$ lb.

It will therefore be seen that a tank 24 in. × 12 in. × 12 in. will contain two cubic feet of water, weighing 125 lb.

Whilst the largest possible surface area is the most desirable, it does not make an attractive tank if the depth is too shallow, so it is best to strike an average. The table will act as a guide to suitable proportions.

When you have decided upon the proportions, you are ready to start making your aquarium. It is a useful thing to remember that you can use either brass or angle iron. Brass is the easier material to work with, iron will require the use of welding plant. However, if iron is preferred, a garage will usually do the welding quite cheaply.

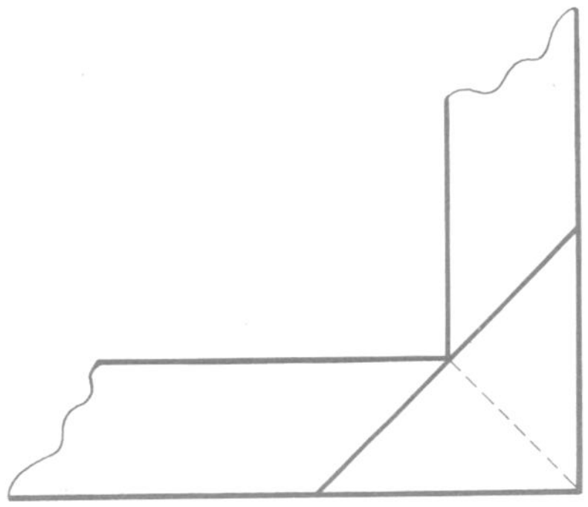

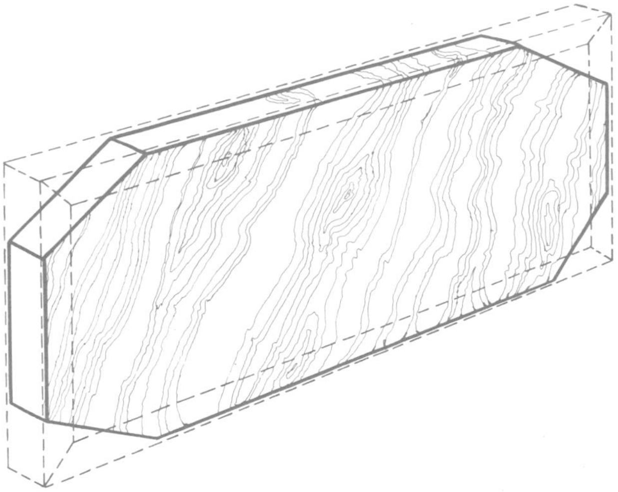

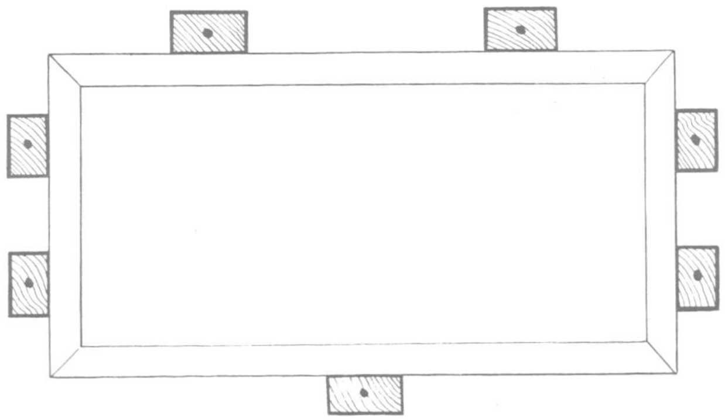

Cut two lengths of brass angle to correspond with the total perimeter, allowing about $\frac{3}{8}$ in. for the bends at the corners. Now mark off the angle to correspond with the lengths of the two sides and two ends. It is best to work from the centre of the angle when marking out, as this method leaves some material at each end for the final sizing after

How to make an aquarium tank

Length in.	*Breadth* in.	*Height* in.	*Angle Iron* in.	*Thickness* in.
16	8	12	$\frac{3}{4}$	$\frac{3}{32}$
18	10	10	$\frac{3}{4}$	$\frac{3}{32}$
24	12	12	1	$\frac{1}{8}$
24	12	15	1	$\frac{1}{8}$
30	12	12	1	$\frac{1}{8}$
36	12	12	1	$\frac{3}{16}$
36	12	15	$1\frac{1}{8}$	$\frac{1}{8}$
38	12	12	$1\frac{1}{4}$	$\frac{1}{8}$
48	12	12	$1\frac{1}{2}$	$\frac{1}{8}$
48	12	15	$1\frac{1}{2}$	$\frac{3}{16}$

the bending has been done. Use a hack saw to cut a 'V' 45° each side of the vertical line that marks the lengths, leaving a small amount of material which you can file away with a flat file. Carry the groove to a depth that leaves a mark on the other side of the angle. This facilitates bending.

The angle is now ready for bending, and this should be executed carefully to prevent the brass cracking in the weakened places.

After bending, cut the two free ends to the correct lengths of side and end, mitre the corners at 45°, and the frame should be a nicely formed rectangle. Repeat with the other length. These two frames will be the base and top of the aquarium.

Thoroughly clean the joints and all the surfaces that will be in contact, treat with flux, and tin with solder.

The corners of the top and bottom frames can now be soldered together, but make sure that the edges naturally contact each other and that no force is required to hold them together.

Additional strength can be obtained if corner brackets are soldered to each corner. It is worth while to make a jig for holding the frames square whilst the soldered joint is made, and you can do this either with a piece of wood cut to the inside dimensions of the frames, or with blocks screwed down to the top of the work-bench after ensuring the corners are square. Do NOT try to press the frames into shape after soldering.

The four uprights can now be cut and filed to the required length. Again ensure that the ends are clean and well tinned with solder. These can now be soldered into the four corners of the bottom frame, making sure that they are perfectly square and upright. A small 'C' clamp can be used to hold them in position until firmly fixed.

The final operation is to solder the top frame in the same manner. Again, a wooden jig can be used. Unless an electric soldering iron is used the tip will cool before it has time to raise the brass to the required temperature to melt the solder. Then a blow lamp or methylated spirit blow torch will be necessary. If you are not particularly expert at soldering, you can drill the uprights and use small screws and nuts to hold the whole frame together until the soldering operation is finished. The screws are then removed and the holes plugged with brass rivets, making sure that the heads are perfectly flat on the inside of the aquarium.

If angle iron is the material chosen, the joints can be made smoother and welding is much stronger than solder. The angle iron should be cut to equal the four lengths, the four ends, and the four uprights, and each end mitred to an angle of 45°. When this is done all ends should fit snugly into each other ready for welding. After the welded joint has been made, the weld can be very carefully hammered to provide a smooth finish.

For aquariums over 30-in. long, I advise an additional stiffener across the centre of the bottom and top frame to prevent bowing of the long sides. Although the bowing may be slight, it is almost certain to cause a leak eventually.

The frame is now ready to be painted in the colour you have chosen. It is better to use a coat of good oil paint rather than synthetic enamels or lacquers, as these tend to chip easily and the chips eventually find their way into the aquarium.

With an iron frame, an undercoat of red lead prevents rust eventually forcing itself through the finished coat of paint.

The inside of the frame should be sparingly painted with gold-size to ensure cohesion between the cement and frame.

If paraffin or gas heating is to be used to maintain the temperature, a slate bottom, or preferably a sheet of fully compressed stipple glazed asbestos (not to be confused with ordinary builders' asbestos), will be necessary. This can usually be supplied by a good builders' merchant, but it is advisable to take along with you a cardboard template of the actual size required. These materials can be sawn, but are very abrasive, so I advise you to use an old saw if you are cutting it yourself.

Once you have finished the frame, you are ready to begin work on the glass. Before putting the glass into the frame, run a smear of gold-size round the edges. This will help to bond it to the cement. The type of glass to be used does not present any problems. The front panel of glass will obviously need to be clear, but the remainder can be horticultural or rough cast.

Glass sizes

Length	Front	Back and Ends	Bottom
Up to 18 in.	24 oz Clear	24 oz Hort.	$\frac{1}{4}$ in. Plate,
Up to 24 in.	32 oz Clear	$\frac{1}{4}$ in. Rough Cast	$\frac{1}{4}$ in. R.C.,
Up to 30 in.	32 oz Clear	$\frac{1}{4}$ in. Rough Cast	or Slate,
Up to 48 in.	$\frac{1}{4}$ in. Plate	$\frac{1}{4}$ in. Plate	or F.C.S.G. Asbestos

The base should have a clearance of $\frac{1}{16}$ in. between the frame and the glass or plate. Spread the cement liberally on the bottom edge of the frame to a thickness of approximately $\frac{1}{4}$ in., making sure that the frame is well covered; lay the glass in and press gently downwards until the cement is about $\frac{1}{8}$ in. in thickness. Clean any surplus cement off with old knife.

Next, treat the two sides in the same manner, and then the two ends. Some aquarists advise wedging the two sides in position with sticks across the inside of the tank, but this method distorts the glass, so that when the sticks are removed it reverts to its natural shape and causes a leak.

The cement usually begins to harden after two or three days, and the aquarium can then be filled with water. The pressure of water will give a final settling to the glass. Make sure that the aquarium is on a firm base which does not rock, before filling. Once your aquarium is filled there is no reason to empty it unless you have to repair a leak, or for some other emergency.

If you decide on a large tank, the bottom should be put in after the two sides, and the ends last. This gives additional strength.

Cements

Aquarium cements should have three qualities—water resistance, adhesiveness, and elasticity, the latter to allow for the slight movement of the glass and frame due to their different coefficients of expansion. Do not use hard cement, because it is almost impossible to remove, and this will make repairs very difficult.

A good quality cement ready for use immediately is now obtainable in tubes and tins. This will, of course, save a fair amount of time and trouble in mixing your own.

The best quality linseed putty is probably the easiest to use. It should be well worked with the hands until quite soft, then liberally pressed into the frame with the fingers, taking particular care to fill the corners.

A slightly better cement can be made if you mix two parts red lead, two parts white lead, and one part putty thoroughly, using a small amount of gold-size to unite the whole mass. To mix the leads with the putty use a board to lay them on, and keep kneading the mixture with a broad putty knife.

Another simple cement is made from equal parts of white lead ground in oil and whiting. The lead and whiting are mixed together with the boiled linseed oil until it reaches the consistency of dough. This mass should then be hung in a muslin bag, much in the same manner as when making cream cheese, and left overnight to set. The next day it should be kneaded again before using. This particular cement has the virtue of remaining soft and in good condition for a considerable time if kept in an airtight tin, and provides a handy standby in an emergency. The more it is kneaded, the softer it becomes.

Should it be necessary to make a quick drying cement, the following formula can be used:

Whiting	16 parts	
Litharge	4 parts	all dry
Powdered red lead	2 parts	
Powdered resin	2 parts	

The ingredients should be mixed together with a good quality varnish to the consistency of a stiff dough. If large areas are to be covered, do not make a large quantity at one time, but make it in small batches as required to prevent the unused cement becoming too hard to work.

Cement containing plaster of Paris should be avoided as it tends to dry rather brittle.

Disinfectants

When the aquarium is completed it should be thoroughly cleansed to ensure that no odd pieces of cement or foreign matter are left inside.

In an old tank that has previously been used for fish, but has not been used for a considerable time, a thorough wash inside with methylated spirits is usually sufficient to remove any dirt or organisms, but with a tank that has been newly made, in addition to the methylated wash, a strong solution of permanganate of potash should be swabbed into the corners and left for a week. The strength of the solution can be judged by colour. If the solution is almost black, then it is the correct strength.

Water

There is a right and wrong way to fill an aquarium.

First ensure that your tank is perfectly flat and does not stand on two corners only. If it is unevenly balanced, the bottom should be packed with small pieces of aluminium or any metal. Cardboard or wood should not be used as the thickness varies with temperature and dampness, and puts an uneven strain on the tank, which will eventually cause a leak or crack the glass.

To fill your aquarium, place a sheet of newspaper on the sand, which has been placed on the bottom of the tank, and pour water gently on to it. The paper will rise with the water level, and prevent a direct stream of water disturbing the sand. A saucer laid on the sand is another method. A water-can with a sprinkler rose provides a good method of filling gently. Do not at any time use hot water as it softens the cement.

Aquaria over 2 ft in length should be filled gradually to allow the glass and frame to settle, and for this reason I advise you to half fill your tank in the morning and finish the job in the evening. It is nearly always best to use old seasoned water. The water should be drawn from the tap and left for a few days to age. It can, of course, be left in the aquarium to season, providing no fish or plants are introduced.

Faults

Leaks are a nuisance, but it is not always necessary to empty the tank to do a repair. The tank should be given a chance to right its own leak. It will often do this provided the seepage is not too fast. A leak rights itself when the suspended matter in the water clogs the fault through which the water is leaking. This process may take up to a week. To prevent a pool of water forming on the floor, attach a strip of newspaper to the underside of the tank just below the leak, this will absorb most of the water before it reaches the floor. When the paper becomes perfectly dry the leak is cured. If, however, it does not stop within a week, the cement should be scraped out between the glass and the frame to a depth of approximately $\frac{1}{4}$ in., a hack saw blade broken in half provides a handy tool for this purpose. If bent back upon itself, the broken edge will have a slight curve that will act as a scoop. Remove the old cement about $1\frac{1}{2}$ in. to each side of the seepage. Next, thoroughly mix red lead with gold-size to a sticky paste. This should be forced down into the crevice with a hack saw blade, or any similar flat tool. When the paste is set, touch it up with paint to match the existing colour.

A really bad leak requires attention from the inside. The aquarium should be emptied and left to dry for at least a week to ensure removal of all the moisture in the cracks, then prop the tank at an angle of about 30° and run gold-size down the inside corners. A small fountain pen filler can be used to apply the gold-size. Do not attempt to use the tank until at least a week after this treatment. A more convenient method is to use a proprietary sealing compound, supplied usually in a tube with a nozzle to make the application simpler. If you prefer this method, ensure that you use a sealer specially made for aquarium use. General type sealers may contain toxic chemicals which are harmful to the fish.

A cracked piece of glass cannot be successfully repaired, the whole pane should be carefully knocked out, old cement removed, and a new piece of glass inserted.

A spare aquarium should always be part of the aquarist's equipment. I know it is a great temptation to use it on one pretext or another, but I advise you to keep it empty of fish so that in the event of an accident it is ready for immediate use.

Heating

To keep tropical fish in the conditions to which they are accustomed, it is necessary to maintain the temperature of the water at an average of 70° to 75°F. There are various ways of doing this according to the facilities at the disposal of the aquarist.

Electrical heating

The easiest and most efficient is the electrical method. The heat is provided by an immersion heater, which is a coil of resistance wire wrapped around a ceramic former, much the same as a bar element of an electric fire. The former is in a heat-resistant glass tube, and sealed with a rubber stopper through which the connecting wires are passed. These heaters can be obtained in various wattages to suit different sizes of tanks.

A thermostat controls the temperature by switching on the heater when it drops below a pre-set figure, and off when the temperature reaches the temperature you require. The thermostat is made of a bimetal strip which has different co-efficients of expansion, causing the strip to bend away from the contact when heat is applied, and vice versa. The thermostat clips over the top edge of the aquarium, and the adjustment of temperature is controlled by a knob which alters the pressure on the strip (see below).

Another type of thermostat has an adjusting screw inside the tube, and a rubber stopper, similar to the heater. This type can be laid on the bottom of the tank. This has the advantage of

allowing you to lower the depth of water for breeding purposes. The disadvantage is that you have to remove it for adjustment. The heater and thermostat are supplied complete. Do not worry if at first the thermostat varies as much as 10°F. Do not try to correct this with the adjusting screw, as this screw only controls the temperature at which the strip will break and make contact. The thermostat should not vary more than ±2°F. If it does, it usually means that the magnet, which ensures a snap action and prevents arcing, is too near the strip, and has some difficulty in making its escape. A quarter turn on the contact screw is usually enough to decrease the pull of the magnet sufficiently to bring it within the required range. The ratio of electrical power to volume of water is 10 watts per gallon of water.

When the contacts of the thermostat make and break, they cause a tiny spark which can cause a disturbance, both to radio and television sets. This can be overcome if a 0·1 microfarad tubular capacitor is connected across the contacts.

To do this, bare the two wires leading from the thermostat as near to the top as possible, and then wrap the capacitor leads around the bared sections, one from each end of the capacitor to each wire, and solder securely.

Make sure the bared portions of wire are then covered completely with insulation tape to avoid a short circuit. A further precaution is to cover the whole capacitor by wrapping insulation tape around the complete assembly.

The type of capacitor used must be of a robust nature, it has to withstand the mains current, therefore it is advisable to tell your dealer the use to which it will be put so that he can give you the correct type.

Another type of heater combines both heating elements and thermostat. The glass tube is mounted vertically in the tank, so that the lower section of the tube containing the heater is well down in the water. This arrangement may be suitable for small tanks, but it probably concen-

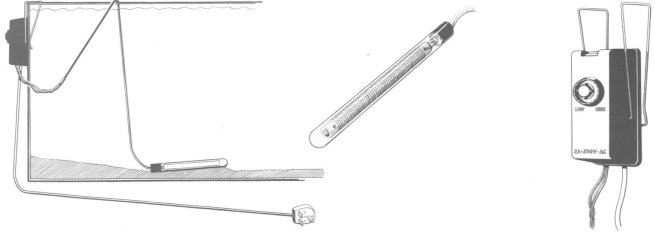

trates the heat energy in too small an area, and too locally.

The flexible heater is another method of electrical heating which is becoming widely used. This consists of a flexible loop containing the element which can be arranged around the inside of the tank, just below the surface of the sand, and is virtually invisible except for the connecting wires.

The choice of equipment is obviously a matter of personal choice, but there is much to recommend two heaters, suitably positioned in the tank to give uniform distribution of heat, and an outside fitting thermostat. These clip on the frame in close proximity to the glass and are easily adjusted for temperature control.

Small aquariums may be heated with an electric light lamp only, with or without a thermostat. I have found from experience that it is not advisable to use this method in a tank over 1 ft. in length, but if you use this method to heat an aquarium which is only used for quarantine or some similar job, it saves the expense of other equipment. The lamp is used in a box, and the aquarium stood on top.

If your tank is 12 in. × 6 in. × 6 in., the outside dimensions of the box will be 12 in. × 6 in., and it will be about 3 in. deep. Line the inside with thin asbestos sheet, and make a few holes for ventilation. Screw a base fixing lamp holder inside— you can use the same screws to hold a strip of aluminium, bent over the bulb to avoid the direct heat of the lamp, which may tend to crack the glass. I have found a 15 watt lamp is sufficient, but in very cold weather a 40 watt lamp is necessary. When you have done this cover the top of the aquarium with a sheet of glass, and *always* have sand on the bottom, otherwise the unnatural position of the light will cause discomfort to the fish.

Oil heating

Although oil heating has been used for tropical tanks for the last 30 years, it has the drawback of not having the ability to be controlled automatically, and needs daily attention. It is possible to obtain standard equipment for this method of heating, but as an alternative you can make your own.

You can get the burners and wick from the local hardware shop. The most satisfactory type of burner has a porcelain insert around the wick, which helps to give a much cleaner flame and cuts down fumes to a minimum. The container should be sufficiently large to hold enough oil to last 24 hours. A sweet or paint tin cut down to 2 in. is ideal, but you should solder the seams and lid to ensure that the joins are sealed, then cut a

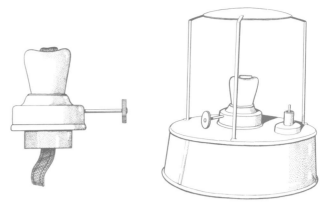

circular hole in the centre of the lid, and insert the burner.

You can make the filler cap from the top of any tin with a screw cap. Cut the top off the tin just below the cap level and solder to the top of the container, first making a hole in the lid to correspond. You can easily provide some indication of the oil level if you make a gauge in the filler cap. To do this, pierce a $\frac{1}{4}$-in. hole in the centre of the cap and solder a short length of copper tube into it, and then cut a piece of $\frac{1}{16}$-in. wire to the depth equal to the distance of the bottom of the container to the top of the $\frac{1}{4}$-in. o/d tube. If you press a cork on to the end of the wire which is inside the container, it will act as a float, and the position of the wire above the tube will tell you the fuel content.

Do not allow a naked flame to come into direct contact with any part of the aquarium, as it will most certainly crack it. It is not difficult to overcome this, if you have a shield of at least $\frac{1}{16}$-in. thick metal fixed directly over the flame. The illustration shows an easy method of doing this.

When using oil as a method of heating, it is advisable to have an experimental run to give some indication of the flame height necessary to maintain the required temperature.

To avoid loss of heat, the bottom of the aquarium can be enclosed in an asbestos skirt or stood on a box similar to that described for heating with an electric light bulb.

Gas heating

Some aquarists use coal gas as a fuel for heating, but as many houses using this type of fuel have a slot meter control, you have to be careful in case the gas supply runs out.

The maintenance of temperature in the methods I have mentioned will, to some extent, be affected by room temperature. The warmer the room, the less additional heat will be required. If you have a thermostatically controlled tank, outside temperature influences will automatically be balanced, but an electric light lamp used without a thermostat requires different wattage bulbs for winter and summer.

There is a cheaper way than supplying electricity to individual tanks. The important question here is whether you can find the space, and want to breed in quantity. If you do, a fish house is the answer. This is cheaper than supplying electricity to individual tanks, all you need is a greenhouse suitably laid out with racks for the tanks, and you can use the boiler system or the electrical unit to maintain the correct temperature.

Temperature

Whatever method of heating is used, its purpose is to maintain a reasonably constant temperature range consistent with the requirement of the fish.

It must be realised that the temperature of the water in an aquarium is not the same throughout; this is because heat rises. The lower regions of the tank will be cooler than just below the surface, quite a few degrees cooler in fact. Fish in natural waters are also subjected to these conditions, therefore it is not unnatural to them. To obtain average temperature readings, the thermometer bulb should be positioned midway between the surface and the bottom.

The majority of thermometers are calibrated in degrees Fahrenheit, and all references in this book are to this scale, but should you wish to convert to degrees Centigrade the following formulæ can be used:

$$(\text{Deg. C} \times 9/5) + 32 = \text{Deg. Fahrenheit}$$
$$(\text{Deg. F} - 32) \times 5/9 = \text{Deg. Centigrade}$$

Lighting

If it were possible to collect daylight, and by some method store and control it in the same manner as we can with electricity, we would have the perfect lighting. Unfortunately, at the time of writing anyway, it is not possible, and we have to resort to means within our scope.

When you choose a position for your aquarium, try to place it so that it will get its fair share of daylight. The light should be diffused, and the tank should receive at least two hours of direct sun each day, which is a minimum if plants are to function properly. If too strong a light penetrates the tank, it will cause the excessive growth of algæ, which takes the form of cloudy green water, mossy growth on the plants, or a green film on the glass, and sometimes a combination of all three. If you have to use very raw water, the actual surface will become coated.

You can control this by shading the aquarium with newspaper, green tinted Cellophane, or by painting the glass sides with a green paint. The shading or cutting down of the light should be treated with caution.

It is better to have too much light than not enough. Algæ is not harmful to fish, but just the opposite. Plants cannot give off oxygen unless they are stimulated by light. But if you can arrange your tank in a position where it will get just the right amount of light, so much the better. There is no formula for this. You obtain the best results by trial and error, and all that is basically required is a little patience.

Artificial light

Artificial light is much the better because you can control the amount of light needed to stimulate the plants, and to some extent prevent the excessive growth of algæ.

The amount of light needed per day for an aquarium measuring 24 in. $\times$ 12 in. $\times$ 12 in., assuming the amount of daylight reaching the tank is negligible, is 50 watts for 9 hours.

It must be remembered that whilst very decorative effects can be obtained by varying the position of the lamps, the source of light should be above the tank so that the rays enter the water in a natural way.

We know that plants must have light if they are to be healthy, so to give them the maximum benefit from artificial lighting, arrange the light source as near to the surface as possible, but take care not to scorch the leaves of tall plants that spread their leaves along the surface.

Fluorescent lighting, which is the subject of much controversy, is, in my experience, practically useless, as the coating on the inside of the tube absorbs most of the infra-red rays.

Aquariums covered with a sheet of glass can be illuminated with a light box, in which one or two lamps are mounted in sockets and stood open side down on the glass. The box should be well ventilated as excessive heat considerably shortens the life of the lamp, and cracks the glass cover. Strip lights in their reflectors can be stood directly on the glass if distance pieces are fixed to each end of the reflector to allow free passage of air around the lamp. The best method is to combine the lighting with a top cover, which screens all extraneous light beams, and illuminates the interior uniformly.

You can buy the tops and covers ready made, but if you wish to make your own, here is the way to do so. It will be easier to describe the construction of the cover if we assume it is for a definite size tank. We will take the most universal size, i.e. 24 in. $\times$ 12 in. $\times$ 12 in. If the cover is required for a tank of different dimensions, it is not a difficult job to make the necessary alterations by drawing the end view to scale, and then measuring it for the new set of figures. The main part will be made from a sheet 21¾ in. $\times$ 14¾ in.

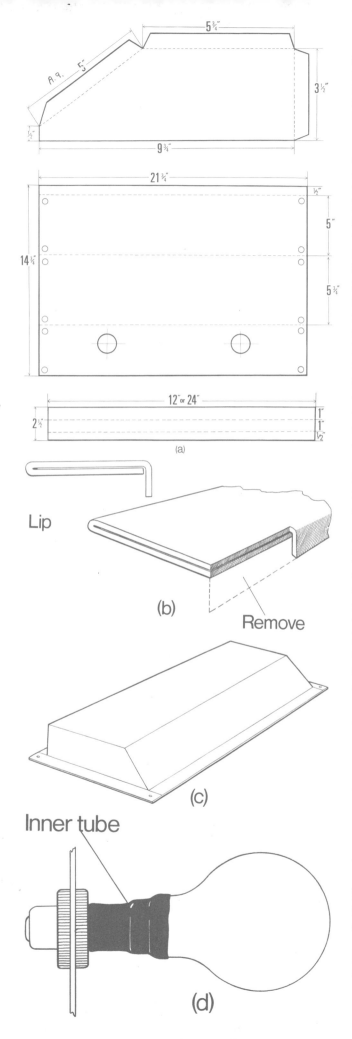

Construction of an aquarium cover
(a) dimensions of the cover and lip
(b) details of the lip
(c) finished cover
(d) lamp mounting

Aluminium is the best material to use, as it is easy to bend and cut, and does not rust. Mark this sheet with a scriber where the bends are to be made (the illustration will show the positions). It will be noted that the length and width dimensions are smaller than the tank dimensions. This is to let the edges sink below frame level by ½ in. inside. Next drill holes for the rivets and the two lamp holders. If a large drill is not to hand, the two large holes can be drilled all round with a smaller drill until the centre falls out and then cleaned up with a half-round file. Now bend along the scribed line to the shape in the illustration and, to ensure a clean bend, sandwich the metal between two strips of hardwood clamped each end with a 'C' clamp. The two ends can now be cut out and the edges turned at right angles. These should now be fitted to the top, drilled through, and riveted.

To make the surrounding lip, cut two strips 2½ in. × 24 in., for the sides, and two 2½ in. × 12 in. for the ends. Mark a line 1 in. back from one edge, and ½ in. from the other. Snick out a piece 1⅛ in. × ½ in. on the ½ in. edge at each end so that when it is bent at right angles it will be the same length as the cover, and leave one inch overlap at each end to be riveted to the side lips. The other edge can now be folded back upon itself to form a double thickness. This will stiffen the whole length. Repeat with the remaining three lengths. These can now be fixed to the main cover. Make sure the bottom edges of the cover and strips coincide, spot through with a drill, and rivet. A final rivet in each corner completes the cover, and the lamp holders can now be assembled through the holes and connected.

One more thing—it is quite likely that condensed water will collect in the lamp holders if left unprotected, and either cause the contacts to arc and burn, or cause a short circuit. However, a piece of cycle inner tube cut to a length of 1½ in. and slipped over the lamp and holder provides an excellent safeguard.

Marine aquaria

Aquaria discussed earlier in this chapter have been specifically related to fresh water tropical conditions, they are, however, totally unsuitable containers for sea water.

Because sea water has a strong corrosive action on metal, marine aquaria should ideally be made entirely of glass, or plastics. Unfortunately, glass tanks of the size required, and with glass fronts free from imperfections caused during moulding, are not readily available. Moulded glass-fibre tanks are becoming available, but they are expensive. Tanks made from wood have been made by keen aquarists for a considerable number of years, and there are some advantages to be gained from this type of construction, but the most practical is still the standard metal frame, glazed with plate glass. Naturally the frame has to be made from a corrosion-proof metal, or has to be suitably protected, and it is possible to obtain tanks with nylon-coated frames, or frames covered with some other suitable plastic.

Tanks manufactured from Plexiglas are also quite suitable except that the material scratches rather easily. For tanks holding over ten gallons of water, the thickness should be $\frac{1}{2}$ in.—anything thinner than this will bow in the course of time owing to the pressure of water, and when setting up the tank the whole area of the base must be supported. On the other hand, Plexiglas does not discolour like most clear plastics and requires little or no maintenance. Cements are important, they should be non-toxic and if possible should not be allowed any contact with the water. If a seam of cement is visible at the glass joints, it is advisable to cover the joint with liquid plastic, black asphaltum varnish, or aqua-scaler.

It may be useful on occasions to use an aquarium that was originally designed for fresh-water. This can be done if the seams, any exposed metal, and the underside of the top of the frame is protected with black asphaltum varnish, or some other suitable insulant.

The aquarium should be thoroughly cleaned and disinfected before it is finally filled. Wash the inside thoroughly with clean water, never use soap or any detergents, and then rub the inside with a damp cloth that has been dabbed in table salt. Wash again, and disinfect with a weak solution of permanganate of potash or, if you prefer, wipe the inside of the tank with methylated spirits, having first dried the interior. Make certain that the underside of the frame and all corners and seams have been fully treated. If you have chosen a metal-framed tank, fill it with fresh water for a few days. The water pressure will cause the cement to thin a little between the glass and frame, and will expose a wider seam inside. Empty the tank by siphoning off, dry the interior and treat the seam with a scaler.

The tank is now ready for siting. Choose the position with some care as once the tank is set up it should not be moved. An ideal position would be near a window facing south, the amount of sunlight falling on to the tank could then be controlled by blinds or by shading with curtains, but if such a position is not available, then try to site the tank where the rays of the sun will fall on to the tank for a period during the day. It may well happen that it is impossible to satisfy either of these suggestions. If this is so, then artificial light will have to be relied upon.

Lebistes reticulatus
Mollienisia latipinna
Xiphophorus maculatus

Plants and layout

An aquarium without plants is like a room without furniture—empty and uninviting.

Even the most exotic fish cannot be shown to advantage in a tank devoid of vegetation, for it is by contrasting the many colours of the fish with a natural background of various shades of green, that we discover the charm of tropical fish.

Photosynthesis

Plants not only provide decoration and a means of simulating natural conditions, they are also functional in the sense that they help to supply oxygen under certain conditions.

All animal life, and this of course includes fish, take in oxygen and expel carbon dioxide. Plants, on the other hand, under the influence of strong light, take in carbon dioxide through their leaves and give off oxygen.

This is an over simplified explanation of photosynthesis, but it does demonstrate the functional aspects of aquarium plants.

As stated previously, oxygenation of the water in an aquarium is far more dependent upon the area of the water exposed to the atmosphere than to the plants it may contain, but the advantage of a well lit and planted tank is in the ability of the plants to absorb some of the carbon dioxide.

It will be appreciated, therefore, that the fish and the plants have some relationship with regard to their capacity to assist in the sustenance of each other, so it is not surprising that planted aquaria without fish rarely prosper.

Before I describe aquarium plants proper, let us consider the medium in which the plants will grow.

Sand

Ordinary builders' sand should not be used because it is difficult to clean and packs tightly, making it hard for plant roots to penetrate, and it does not allow the water to circulate. The best sand can be bought washed ready for use. However, it should be washed again just before you put it into your aquarium, as it is certain to have collected a quantity of dust whilst in store. This sand

Xiphophorus hellerii

is really fine grit of a pebbly texture, ranging in size from about $\frac{1}{16}$ in. to $\frac{1}{8}$ in. It should not be larger as bits of uneaten food may fall between and cause the water to foul. It is also worth noting that any large stones put into the tank for decorative effect should be pressed well into the sand for the same reason.

The depth of sand can be varied to suit your individual taste, but for general purposes I have found a 2-in. layer of sand ideal.

The sand should be thoroughly washed with successive rinses of water, and stirred until the water remains clear when the sand is disturbed. It should then be boiled in a bucket to ensure that no germs are introduced into the tank, and washed again. This may seem a trifle fastidious, but it means that when the tank is finally set up, your aquarium will be in a healthy state and, if you take reasonable care when you introduce new plants and fish, it will remain healthy. Do not be tempted to put a layer of earth under the sand in the mistaken idea that it will assist the plants to grow. It does not work out in practice.

Remember the fish provide nourishment needed by the plants, but if the temptation is too great to overcome, and you feel you must experiment, use potting compost or clay, or try a mixture of one third peat, one third clay and one third coarse sand—this planting medium has the advantage of being proven, to some extent, by Dutch aquarists. However, if you are experiencing your early days of fish-keeping, start with sand, it is much safer, and remember—under no circumstances use garden soil.

Attractive presentations and lay-outs can be effected by sloping the sand from about 4 in. at the back of the aquarium to about $1\frac{1}{2}$ in. at the front, or any other gradient that is pleasing and practical. Such an arrangement shows the plants to better advantage, and encourages the sediment to drift to the lower level, at the front of the tank, where it can be easily siphoned off.

There is a minor problem in retaining the sandy slope if it is steep, because of the natural tendency of sand to flatten out when saturated with water. This can be overcome by pressing strips of thin Perspex vertically into the sand to form barriers,

19

and concealing them with a further layer of sand.

When you are planting or doing any other work in your aquarium which disturbs the base and makes the water cloudy, you will discover when it settles that it leaves a thin dirty film over the top of the sand. Siphon this off.

Fertilising

Leave fertilising to the fish; they will provide all that is necessary. If the plants are not doing well it is probably through insufficient light, or perhaps they are bunched too closely together.

If the aquarist is interested in experimenting, he must be careful of the fertiliser used. W. T. Innes recommends a liquor made from pulverised sheep's manure and shooting it into the sand about the roots by using a pippet tube. Frankly, I have never found it necessary or desirable to fertilise, but prefer to find a cause for the trouble, rather than introduce another element into the tank.

Planting

Before putting new plants into your tank it is just as well to ensure that they are clean and free from germs and unwanted snails. To do this, rinse them under the tap and remove any yellow or decaying leaves, and also remove any of the jelly-like eggs of snails you may find on the leaves. They can then be immersed in a solution of concentrated lime water diluted with water to a proportion of six parts tap water to one part lime water. To make lime water, liberally mix hydrated lime in water and let the sediment settle, then draw off the clear water and mix as previously described.

The plants should be left in the solution for 10 minutes, no more, and then placed in a solution of permanganate of potash for a like period. The strength of the potash should be a quarter grain to a gallon.

It is important never to allow the plants to get dry whilst they are in transit, or at any other time. They should be wrapped in several layers of newspaper soaked in water with a final wrapping of greaseproof to prevent evaporation.

When adding plants to the tank after it has been filled, a pair of planting sticks will be found useful. Push the plant into the sand with one of the sticks, and heap sand around the roots with the other. The sticks can be made by splitting a bamboo cane or any thin strip of wood, and sandpapering it smooth. A 'V' notched in the end of one will allow stray root strands to be pushed well into the sand.

If plants are not firmly anchored into the sand, their buoyancy causes them to rise to the surface. Plants with small roots can be anchored temporarily with thin strips of lead wound around their base. Do not squeeze the lead so hard that it will bruise or injure the delicate structure of the plants. If the roots become black through contact with the lead, or any other reason, you can return them to their natural colour by floating them in water exposed to strong sunlight for 24 hours.

Plants should never be bunched closely together. They should be planted to allow water and light to reach the stems. Closely packed roots can form a trap for sediment.

When obtaining new plants, it is best to select them about half-grown rather than more developed specimens which have reached or even surpassed their best.

Plants covered with algæ should be avoided, the algæ chokes the plants and tends to spread.

Plants

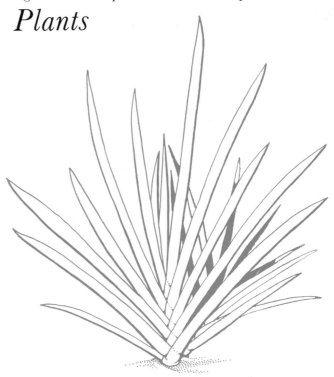

Acorus gramineus var. pusillus (Japanese dwarf rush)

As its name implies, this is one of the smaller plants that is ideal for placing near the front of the aquarium. The leaves are narrow and grow to 2 or 3 in. only. It does require strong light if it is to prosper, but it grows quite slowly. It can be divided into smaller plants by carefully splitting from the rhizome, or root base.

Anubias lanceolata (water aspidistra)

The water aspidistra is an unusual aquarium plant which was discovered in French Guinea some 30 years ago.

It is an aspidistra-like plant with thick glossy green leaves which are about 6-in. long, supported

by short, strong stems, and will grow well in weak light.

Propagation is by division of the root stock.

Aponogeton crispum

A. crispum is a delightful plant to use as a key piece from which to plan the balance of the 'under-water landscape'. The leaves are pale green in colour and so delicate that they are almost trans-lucent. The margins are crinkled, not unlike some species of seaweed. The slim stems will extend their length to suit the water depth, an ideal depth being about 12–15 in. This plant does, however, need a strong light.

It is a species found naturally in Ceylon, and can be propagated by division of the root stock.

Aponogeton fenestrale (Madagascar lace plant)

The Madagascar lace plant is a unique plant. The leaves grow to about 16-in. long and about 3½-in. wide, and join the root by short stems.

The unique feature of this plant is the leaf struc-ture, which consists of a skeleton-like lattice of veining like crochet lace. Although delicate in structure, the leaves are much tougher than they appear.

Aponogeton fenestrale is a very desirable decora-tive addition to any aquarium, but it has two main disadvantages—it is usually expensive and it does not grow readily, therefore aquarists who are not experienced should save their money as it is un-likely that they will be successful in growing it.

Propagation is by splitting the root stock, and by seeds.

Aponogeton undulatus

This plant has long blade-like leaves with un-dulating edges, and grows to about 20 in. in good light. It is mainly a decorative plant, but it is a poor oxygenator.

Bacopa amplexicaulis

Bacopa is an attractive aquarium plant with stout round stems that stand vertical in water. The small ovate leaves are attached by short stems to the main stem for the entire length of the plant. It can be used most effectively if a few stems are planted together. It grows best at a temperature of about 68°F but will stand higher temperatures.

It can be propagated by cuttings, which will readily root.

B. monnieria is a similar species which is also suitable for aquaria.

Cabomba caroliniana (fanwort)

This is also known as watershield. The main attraction of *Cabomba* is its delightful appearance. The leaves are light green in colour and spread out in fan-like form from a central stem, and provide a good retreat for young fish. *Cabomba* is not particularly good for spawning, as the leaves are not sufficiently dense.

When planting you should remove the foliage for about 2 in. from the bottom end of the stem to make sure no leaves are buried in the sand to become a potential source of decay.

Cabomba is one of the plants which can be bunched, but not too tightly. If they are tied together with a thin strip of lead when you buy them, the ends should be broken off, and there will then be a good chance for the stems to take root.

This plant is not particularly hardy or a good oxygenator and should be considered mainly as a decoration.

C. caroliniana rosaefolia is a rosy red variety that can be used to contrast with the general greenness of most aquarium plants.

These can be propagated from cuttings.

Ceratophyllum (hornwort)

Ceratophyllum, or hornwort, could become an exhibit in almost every tank, but unfortunately it has two main drawbacks. The leaves are so brittle that they snap off at the slightest touch, and it has no real roots.

The leaves resemble *Myriophyllum* in structure, except that they are coarser. I do not advise its use in an exhibition tank, but it is useful for breeding if it is weighted down with small pieces of lead.

If left floating in an aquarium, thin, tendril-like shoots grow from the stem towards the sand in an attempt to root.

It can be propagated from cuttings.

Ceratopteris thalictroides (Indian fern)

First introduced as an aquarium plant in the 1930s, *C. thalictroides*, or Indian fern, to give it its popular name, is a plant which is used to tropical zones and flourishes best in a temperature of above 70° F.

The leaf formation is unmistakably fern-like, the submerged fronds being attached to stems that are rather brittle, and rise from a crown.

If planted in deep water, the stems may reach a length of a few feet. In shallow water the leaves will either float just below the surface, or extend themselves above the surface and bear a fine cluster of rather coarse foliage.

This is a plant that grows readily in artificial light, which, in my opinion, is the best way to grow it.

Young plants pressed into the sandy bottom of the aquarium, and given the right amount of heat and light, will soon grow into strong plants.

It is just as well to replace old plants occasionally with younger ones, as the old plants will turn brown with decay. Snails find them good to eat, so you have to replace the plants at fairly frequent intervals.

For propagation *C. thalictroides* develops a perfect miniature of itself among the foliage. These miniatures then detach themselves and float to the surface. This, however, does not generally happen until part of the leaf or frond has turned brown and withered away. The young plants can then be collected and planted where required.

Cryptocoryne (water trumpet)

Here we have an individualist in aquatic plants. The beautifully shaped leaves have a particular fascination of their own. The *Cryptocorynes* are not lovers of strong light, so if your aquarium is placed in a shady position, these are the plants to use, but it is well to remember that they do require some light stimulus, so do not overdo the shading. Because the quantity of light required for *Cryptocoryne* is less than most aquatics it is obviously better to use only plants of this nature in one tank, otherwise you have to compromise between supplying strong light for some plants, and a weaker light for others, and end up satisfying neither.

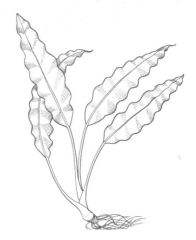

Cryptocoryne cordata

The leaf form of this plant is similar in shape to *C. griffithii*, except for the edges which undulate, but are not crinkly.

If you inspect closely you will see that the leaf colouring is an olive green with a touch of rusty brown, and the inside has a strong red tint. The veining is well marked.

It grows to an average length of 10 in., and propagates in the same way as the *willisii*.

These plants are naturally tropical, and they should be kept in a temperature ranging between 70° and 80° F.

Cryptocoryne beckettii

This is a very small plant. In fact, it is the smallest of the family. The leaves, a delicate green and sword-like, tend to grow in a horizontal position, giving the plant an untidy look. They grow to about 6 in.

Cryptocoryne griffithii

This is a native of Malaya. The leaves attain a length of 10 in. and have a crinkly appearance. They are dark green in colour, with a reddish underside.

Cryptocoryne ciliata

This is a typical *Cryptocoryne* species of plant, the stems hold together giving a strong vertical effect, which is useful for 'landscaping'. It has the advantage of not minding a little salt in the water, as it is found naturally in brackish waters.

Cryptocoryne willisii

This is probably the most popular of the *Cryptocorynes*. The leaves have a wavy edge and are a bright medium green in colour. Propagation is by means of a short runner or small plants broken off from the mother plant. Once they are established they should not be removed unnecessarily as they have an objection to new locations. They grow to an average length of 6 in.

Echinodorus intermedius (Amazon sword)

This, in my opinion, is the best of the bunch—the real aristocrat of the aquarium. The 18-in. leaves sprout from a large crown in a plume-like spray, making an artistic base from which to plan the remainder of the aquarium. The thin translucent leaves are a beautiful fresh green, tapering down towards the crown to form a shortish stem.

It propagates from long runners, which should be pressed down into the sand where new plants begin to develop. It can also be propagated by breaking down a large plant into smaller ones.

The lighting for the Amazon sword should be good, but not too powerful. A little daylight helps, but is not essential.

Egeria densa

Egeria is also known by the name of *Anacharis*, and is a similar type to *Cabomba*, having leaves attached to running stems. Whilst *Egeria* is at its best in a partially protected outside pool, it can be used quite successfully in the aquarium. One of its main attractive features is that is is a quick growing plant—a growth of 1 in. in a day is not unusual. The closely packed leaves, like *Cabomba*, offer a hide-out to young fish, but the leaves are too coarse for spawning tropical fish.

The early aquarists considered this plant to be one of the best oxygenators, but judged by present-day standards they seem to be wrong. But I do not advise you to exclude it from your selection on that account, as it makes an interesting specimen if only for the speed of its growth.

It can be propagated from cuttings.

Normally, *Egeria* is only suitable for cold-water aquariums, but a species *E. densa*. var. *crispa* is suitable for either tropical or cold water. The stem and leaves are shaped the same as *E. densa*, except that they bend back upon themselves, and form a curly pattern.

E. densa var. *longifolia* is a tropical plant from Brazil which is best suited to tropical aquaria. It is similar to *E. densa*, but the leaves are longer.

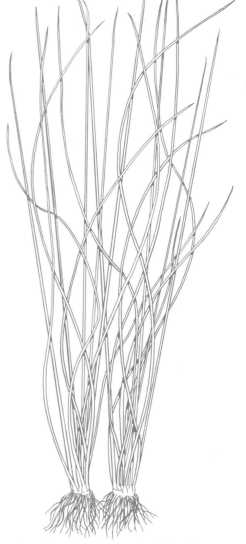

Eleocharis acicularis (hairgrass)

Eleocharis is probably better known as hairgrass, and is an excellent plant to use for adding the finishing touch to a well-laid-out aquarium. The best effect can be obtained by planting it near to a rock. The thin hair-like leaves reach an average length of 5 in., and look their best when planted in a thick clump, although care must be taken to ensure that water and light can freely reach the base of the leaves, otherwise they turn yellow and decay. Thickets formed in this way provide an excellent retreat for baby fish.

It propagates by runners in a similar way to *Vallisneria*.

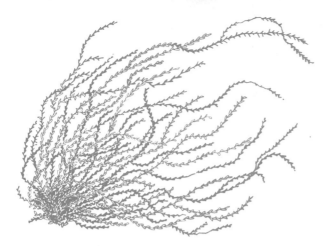

Fontinalis gracilis (willowmoss)

Fontinalis gracilis is a plant with long tendril-like stems covered with tiny pale green leaves. It is a native plant that likes to attach itself to submerged stones, or pieces of waterlogged wood, but it is not too easily found in our streams. However, it is a plant that will do well in the tropical aquarium, and once established it will spread rapidly to provide an excellent medium for fish that spawn on plants at the bottom of the aquarium.

If *F. gracilis* is taken from a stream it will be found to harbour many tiny water creatures, usually crustacea, and although these creatures provide excellent pickings for the adult Siamese fighter, it is safer to wash the plant thoroughly before introducing it into your aquarium.

Hygrophila polysperm

This is a species that has the appearance of a terrestrial plant, and it is particularly interesting because it is the only aquatic of the genus. The leaves sprout from a central stem not unlike the foliage of antirrhinum, except that the colouring is much lighter. It propagates from cuttings snipped off just below a node with outgrowing root tendrils on the stem.

Limnophila (Ambulia)

Ambulia is a similar type of plant to *Cabomba*, the main differences being in the shape of the leaf. The difference is that the fan-shaped leaves

of *Cabomba* form a semicircle, but the leaves of *Ambulia* form a complete circle.

The smaller leaves are bunched rather close together, making it one of the ideal spawning plants. Of Indian origin, it has been a well-sought-after plant for aquarium use since 1932.

It can be propagated by cuttings. Smallish shoots snipped off from where they join the main stem make the best plants.

Ludwigia mulerttii (marsh loosetife)

Ludwigia is not a true aquatic, but is really a bog plant. The leaves are similar in shape to privet leaves, and plenty of light is necessary for growth. If you plant it in a shady part of the aquarium, the leaves will droop.

It is easily propagated by snicking off a piece of plant just where the leaves join the stem, and you can see the young tendrils shooting. You can then plant the cutting in the normal way.

L. palustris is the only British species.

Myriophyllum (water milfoil)

Here is a plant of delicate fern-like beauty, and the thin abundant leaves, which are attached to a central stem, form a perfect spawning plant. It floats naturally just below the surface, which is ideal as a protection for young livebearers, and if you use them to catch the eggs of spawning fish you should plant in a thick cluster.

If used normally, the stem should be stripped in the same manner as *Cabomba* before planting.

tive leaves are supported **on firm st**ems which spread out from the root b**as**e (**rhizom**e).

Nuphar is best planted **in water at** a depth not less than 6 in., and no **deeper than** about 14 in. As the plant is somewhat **buoyant, it** should be set firmly into the sand. **Light is not a v**ery important factor in growing this **plant, but so**me, of course, is necessary.

A few species are **of Europea**n and Asiatic origin, but most of the **species are N**orth American.

M. *alterniflorum* is a British species, and like all the *Myriophyllums* it needs constant replanting and pruning.

M. *pinnatom* is a species from North and South America, and it is a red-bronze colour. M. *lippuroides* is a species from North America that is likely to turn red or brownish-red if subjected to strong and ample lighting, this probably is the reason for its common name 'red myriophyllum'.

Nitella gracilis

Nitella gracilis is native to the British Isles and North America. It is a plant more suited to cold water, but it is an adaptable plant that soon acclimatises to the tropical aquarium.

It is a delicate, pretty plant that has no roots, nevertheless, it grows rapidly in an aquarium that is well illuminated, and it is a good oxygenator. It is better suited to aquariums containing small fish, but it also provides an excellent refuge plant if grown in reasonably dense clumps. It is also useful when breeding egg-layers, as it can be laid flat along the bottom of the aquarium and retained with small round stones to provide a natural egg trap, and protection for fry when they hatch.

Nuphar (spatterdock)

Nuphar is an ideal plant to use as a 'feature' in the planting arrangement. It has large, long leaves which are membraneous and coloured a delicate, translucent light green. These attrac-

Sagittaria (arrowhead)

Sagittaria is a similar plant to *Vallisneria*. The name *Sagittaria* is derived from the arrow-like form of the leaves, causing it to be named after Sagittarius, the mythological archer.

There are three main species, *Sagittaria natans*, *S. gigantea*, and *S. subulata*.

Sagittaria natans is a moderate sized plant, and well suited to tanks of about 12 in. in depth. The leaves usually reach a length of between 6 in. and 9 in. This plant is not confined to tropical aquaria, and has been for many years used by goldfish fanciers.

Sagittaria gigantea, as its name suggests, is a much larger plant, averaging 15 in. in length, and the leaves are $\frac{1}{2}$ in. or more in width. When well rooted, they are sturdy and will stand quite a lot of knocking from your net when you are chasing your fish.

Sagittaria subulata differs from the other two species in various respects. The colour is a darker green, and the leaves have a much straighter form and are usually slightly thicker.

Sagittaria lorata is another species suitable for aquarium use. The oval or oblong leaves float along the surface.

It can be propagated by runner in a similar way to *Vallisneria spiralis*. *Sagittaria* should not be planted in the same aquarium as *Vallisneria*, however, as they rarely do well when together.

It has been noticed with *Sagittaria* that when the aquarium is broken down for replanting, the sand is still clean and sweet, which indicates that the plant roots actually help to purify the sand.

Sertularia cupressina (sea cypress)

Although sea cypress is not truly a plant, its use in the aquarium justifies its being included under this heading.

Sea cypress is, in fact, the external skeleton of a hydroid polyp. It is found naturally in the tidal waters of Holland, Germany, Iceland and Great Britain and along the coasts of the North Sea. In this state it has a mossy, delicate appearance. It grows on the sea bed, sometimes in bunches or beds up to 10 in. in depth.

The skeleton is made of chitin—the same substance that forms the outer case of insects. The inhabitants are removed by a process of washing and drying, which leaves the skeleton clean and more or less dehydrated. It is in this form that it is procurable for the use of aquarists. When dropped into an aquarium the 'feathers' spread out to make a life-like ornamental plant.

If a single 'feather' is viewed under a low power microscope, the little pockets that once housed the tiny polyp can be seen quite clearly.

Sea cypress can be used in the aquarium simply to make a decorative piece, but its real value lies in its use as a breeding 'plant'.

When used as a breeding plant it is not necessary to cover the bottom of the aquarium with sand. The cypress can be anchored with a small piece of lead attached by squeezing to the base. The buoyant stems will then flow upwards, making an ideal egg catcher or refuge for livebearers.

Another advantage of sea cypress is the fact that it can be stored when dry in a paper bag, and seems to last indefinitely if handled carefully. It is just the thing to keep handy when natural plants are difficult to obtain.

After using for a particular spawning, sea cypress can either be washed gently under a running tap and returned to the aquarium, or thoroughly dried and stored.

It is also known as sea moss and white weed.

Vallisneria spiralis (eel or tape grass)

Vallisneria spiralis is also known by the names of eel grass, tape grass, and channel grass. This plant is a firm favourite of most aquarists, and certainly one of mine. It is a tall plant, and well suited to

form a background for the smaller ones. It is, in fact, just the plant one would expect to find in an under-water scene. The tall, grass-like leaves are a light green in colour and rise vertically from the crown to the top of the water, where they float along the surface.

One of the best oxygenators, *Vallisneria spiralis* also has the virtue of being easy to grow. The method of propagation is by runners. These runners grow out from the crown along the sand, and new plants shoot up from the ends of them. It is possible in a well-established tank to remove a plant and find a whole string of them connected together. It is, therefore, advisable when removing plants of this nature from the aquarium to snip the runners before actually removing the plant.

The species are separate, either male or female. The female flowers are on long stems which reach to the surface. The male flowers are attached to the base of the leaves, which, when ripe, become detached and rise to the surface, where they float among the females fertilising them. The stem of the female flower coils up spirally under water, and it is from this that the name is derived.

Do not cover the crown with sand when planting, leave about $\frac{1}{8}$ in. free.

V. torta is a variation of *V. spiralis*. The somewhat broader translucent leaves twist in a slow twirl like a corkscrew, and this plant is probably better known as 'corkscrew val'. This species does not grow so tall as *V. spiralis*. *V. spiralis* var. *gigantea* is an extremely large variety growing up to 6 ft. under favourable conditions, with leaves between $\frac{1}{2}$ in. and 2 in. in width. It thrives in tropical aquaria in which a temperature of 85°F is maintained.

Floating plants

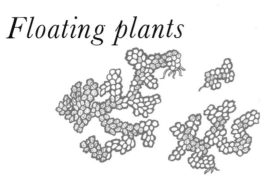

Azolla (fairy moss)

Not too common in this country, *Azolla* has a slightly smaller leaf than duckweed and in formation reminds one of a magnified snow crystal.

The colouring is sage green, varying to a dull red. This plant is also known as water or fairy moss.

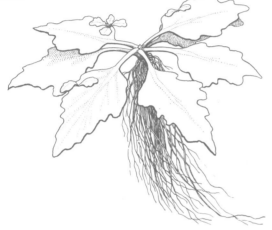

Ceratopteris pteroides (water fern)

C. pteroides is popularly known as floating fern, and comes from South America. It is one of the largest floating plants.

The thick mat provided by the submerged roots is ideal for some species to spawn. Siamese fighters, for example, like to spawn under the leaves. It also provides a haven for young livebearers.

The pretty rosette-shaped plant can grow to a large diameter under favourable conditions, and is usually seen covered with a mass of young plants which form on the larger parent plant leaves.

As it requires a humid atmosphere, it grows better in a covered aquarium, where no direct rays from the lights can dry or scorch it.

It is a good idea to remove any snails from a tank containing this plant; they are rather inclined to make a meal of it.

Eichhornia crassipes (water hyacinth)

Eichhornia crassipes is a very attractive plant, but should be reserved only for large aquaria. In its natural environment in the Gulf States it grows

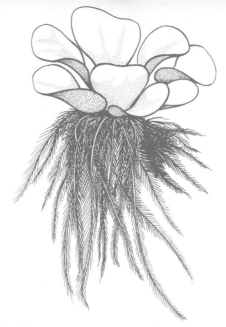

prolifically to the extent of being a nuisance to navigation.

The plant floats on the water surface, with dark bushy roots suspended below. This root mass is very useful for breeding species of fish that drop adhesive eggs near the surface. The leaves of *E. crassipes* are a shiny green, and grow in the shape of rosettes. The plant obtains its buoyancy from swellings in the leaf stem near the root. The swellings are filled with a sponge-like tissue.

The hyacinth-like flower, which is lavender coloured, will bloom under the stimulus of bright light, but it will only last a matter of hours.

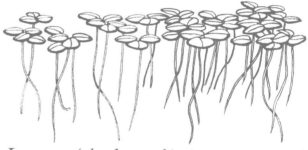

Lemna (duckweed)

Duckweed is a common sight around the edges of our ponds and lakes, forming a green mantle which, from a distance, is easily mistaken for scum. This is almost certain to be *L. minor*, and is suitable for both heated and unheated aquaria.

These dainty little floating leaves make a rather pretty roof for an aquarium and can be used to cut down light. A strange thing about this plant is the fact that it does not seem to prevent or impair the surface of the water from absorbing oxygen from the atmosphere. When obtaining *Lemna* from natural waters, remember that it is likely to harbour considerable small life, some of which are definitely undesirable characters, including hydras and trematodes. Really cleanse the plants before putting them into an aquarium containing fish.

There are 12 species of this genus, four of which are native. *L. trisulca* (ivy leafed duckweed) is probably the most attractive, being a miniature replica of ivy. It will not die in a poor light, but will grow much better if subjected to strong light. It is an ideal plant for keeping the water really clear.

You will find duckweed an asset in your aquarium, but bear in mind that it tends to be difficult to control in an outdoor pond.

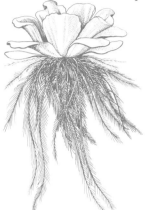

Pistia stratiotes (water lettuce)

Pistia stratiotes is normally a tropical plant and likes plenty of moist heat. Aquariums with a raised top cover and lights built in are not ideal for this plant, as they tend to dry the leaves, which then go white.

The light green, fluted, velvety leaves spread out from the centre like the petals of a flower, and under suitable conditions will reach a diameter of 4 in.

The roots provide a spawning ground for the surface egg layers, but are not dense enough to be ideal.

It propagates by surface runner, and prefers shallow water.

Riccia fluitans (crystalwort)

This is probably the most useful of all the floating plants. It is equally useful for holding the spawn of surface egg layers and sufficiently penetrable to provide a retreat for young livebearers.

Riccia forms a tangled mat of interlocking fibre-looking greenery, sometimes to a thickness of $\frac{3}{4}$ in. It should not be allowed to get any thicker, otherwise it will decay through lack of light and free passage of water.

Owing to the closely packed formation of *Riccia*, it is difficult to keep clean of algæ, but plenty of snails will hold it in reasonable bounds.

Care should be taken not to include ramshorns with the collection of snails. They just love to make a meal of it.

A really good oxygenator, it multiplies by separation; one part separates from the parent and becomes a parent itself, and so on.

Salvinia natans

This is a floating plant resembling duckweed, except for the shape of the leaf, which is heart-shaped. The top surface of the leaf is covered with fine hairs giving a soft velvety appearance and the roots are quite long.

This plant is not ranked among the best oxygenators.

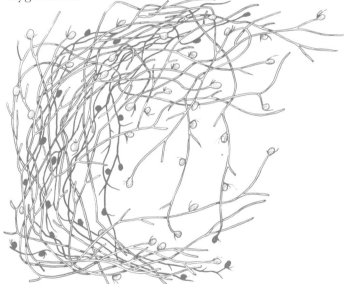

Utricularia (lesser bladderwort)

Bladderwort is a plant which resembles a tangled mass of light green cotton, with little knots attached to the strands, as if someone has tried to untangle it and lost patience. The knot-like appendages are little bladders which trap micro-organisms.

This plant is ideal for spawning surface egg layers and as a protective maze for very young livebearers, being even of a closer formation than *Riccia*.

When using bladderwort it is advisable not to have any other floating plants in the same tank, as they will become hopelessly entangled with each other.

29

Rocks

When selecting rocks remember your aquarium should represent, as near as possible, a natural picture of underwater life. Rocks of multishape and colour should never be put in the same tank, as they are unlikely to be found naturally mixed.

Rocks can be made to form arches, terraces, and to hold banks of sand at higher levels. They are, in effect, the foundation stones of a well laid-out aquarium. It is not, of course, essential to have any rock in the tank. Some very attractive scenes can be designed with plants alone.

My own two favourites are Cumberland stone and the greenish-brown, flat, slatey-looking rocks found in Devonshire streams. These flat natural pieces can either be pressed into the sand to form a high pinnacle, or laid flat and built up one upon the other to form a natural-looking ledge.

Weather-worn pieces are the best, but try to avoid rocks with jagged protrusions, as they may cause injury to your fish.

I have already mentioned the importance of avoiding nooks and crannies where uneaten food can pollute and sediment collect, but I make no excuse for repetition. If after the rocks and stones have been sited to your liking there are any of these pockets, fill them in completely with sand.

As a safeguard, scrub all new pieces with a hard bristle brush and water to remove any dirt, then boil. Avoid using rocks of a soft or synthetic nature; these become soluble in water.

If you have a piece of doubtful rock, put it in a bucket of clean water for a few days, if an oily ring appears on the surface, do not use it.

Although I would not recommend it, it is possible to make rocks to suit your own taste, using cement and sand. After the rocks have been moulded to the required design, and steps have been taken to ensure that no sharp projections have been left, leave for about a week to thoroughly harden. Then boil for at least an hour, which will remove most of the free lime. Next soak the 'rock' in a strong solution of permanganate of potash for about six hours. In addition to disinfecting the rock, it also adds to the appearance by making it look more natural and weathered. A final soak under a running tap for an hour and the rock is ready for use.

Layout

Layout will, of course, be governed mostly by personal taste and artistic ability, but to those setting up their first tank the suggestions with regard to numbers of plants, etc. may be useful.

The heater should never be buried in the sand, as this may cause a deposit of lime to form around the glass tube and impair its efficiency. It is better to wrap lead around each end of it to overcome the tendency to buoyancy, and stand it on two small flat stones to allow free passage of water all round it. It is also easier to remove sediment with a siphon if the heater does not rest on the sand.

When the single heater is used, the best position is in the centre of the tank, but near the back as it can then be hidden from view by a piece of rock.

Avoid moulding the interior in such a manner that everything is symmetrical. A rock right in the centre of the tank with an equal number of plants each side is a sorry sight, and will certainly not look natural; neither will a large heavy rock tucked tightly into a corner without any obvious balancing piece.

The aquarium should look balanced. The illustration shows a well laid-out tank, the rock slightly off-set to the left together with a largish Indian fern plant, are balanced by the tall Amazon sword on the extreme right, with a uniform background of *Vallisneria* or *Sagittaria*.

The attractiveness of the aquarium can be greatly enhanced if the sandy bottom is made to undulate. A method has been described on page 19 to produce a sloped bed, but more ambitious and realistic effects can result from the combined use of stones and sand. First make the foundation using stones about the size of your hand, and place them so that they support each other, fill in the spaces with smaller stones so that they interlock firmly, then finally fill in with sand. Remember that it will be necessary to add plants, so make provision for suitable pockets of sand in your arrangements.

Keep everything in proportion. The use of too large pieces of rock, for example, gives a false impression of depth. When you are planting, group the species together as most unnatural effects will be the result of single specimens dotted about in a haphazard manner. Also, remember to put the tallest plants at the back of the tank so that the view from the front is not obscured.

How many plants will you need in a tank measuring 24 in. × 12 in. × 12 in.? It depends on how many fish are intended to live in the tank. The maximum number of fish of an average size of 2-in. long that should be put in is 35. This is only an average figure, as some fish can stand more crowding than others. Guppies, for instance, can stand up to about 80 in a tank of this size. However, we will consider the tank as holding its full complement of fish. The number of plants required is as follows:

18 *Vallisneria* ..	..	..	12-in. long
2 Indian fern	..	..	Large
1 Amazon sword	..	..	Medium
6 *Ambulia* ..	..	..	Medium
or:			
18 *Sagittaria* ..	..	..	12-in. long
2 *Cabomba* ..	..	..	12-in. long
8 *Myriophyllum*	..	..	12-in. long

Hair grass, etc. can be added for effect. The above number of plants is not intended to be a rigid rule, but a guide for the beginner.

Setting up a marine aquarium

Aquaria, sea water, feeding and fish, for the marine aquarium have been briefly covered under their appropriate headings.

The siting of a marine aquarium is reasonably important. If subjected to strong sunlight, it has a tendency to turn green very fast, so find a corner protected from the direct rays of the sun.

The floor of the tank should be covered with the usual aquarium sand—well washed, of course—but unfortunately plants cannot be introduced. There is no known marine vegetation that will prosper in such confinement, therefore the furnishing is limited to rocks, shells, corals and stones. Remember always to boil them in water before introducing them into the tank.

Continual aeration and filtration is an essential requirement, so fit a suitable airlift-type filter.

Having prepared the 'home' for our marine fish, all that is necessary then is to introduce the fish. But it is very important to limit the number of fish to about 8 or 10 in a 20-gallon aquarium, assuming the fish are about 2-in. long. There are not many good citizens among the marine fish community.

Aquarium Management

Green water

Green water in itself is not necessarily an evil. It is a form of plant life which oxygenates the water in the same way as other leaf plants. Its drawback is, of course, that it prevents you from seeing clearly what is actually happening in the aquarium.

The green colouring in the water is the result of microscopic vegetable cells that need light and food to develop in the same way as all living matter. If you remove the light, you get rid of the green water, but the problem is not as easy to solve as that. Fish and plants need light to live. The solution is a compromise; you have to cut down the amount of light, and apart from advising you to do this, I cannot give you a hard and fast rule to cover all cases of green water as it is a condition which requires individual treatment. My own tanks, for example, sometimes prove the inconsistency of the development of green water. I have experimented with three tanks receiving exactly the same amount of light, quantity of food, and with the same number of plants in each one. Suddenly one of them has taken on the faint green hue so familiar to aquarists.

As a quick remedy, I have found that a large quantity of daphnia tipped into the tank clears it in a few hours. When you do this, remove the fish first as daphnia is an oxygen breather and, if a large number is used, it will almost exhaust the supply of free oxygen in the water.

Aquaria with plenty of strong healthy plants, and not overcrowded with fish, keep the cleanest. Slightly acid water tends to keep water clean, but has the disadvantage that it discourages plant growth.

A mantle of duckweed, *Salvinia*, or *Riccia* will aid in cutting down the amount of light. Even if the water is only a faint green it is advisable to take this action, but be careful to keep the feeding down to a minimum until this condition is cleared up.

Cloudy water

Cloudy water with a slightly muddy appearance is another proposition altogether, for while green water is healthy, opaque mistiness of a grey colour is a danger signal as it is caused by an excess of organic matter in the water, probably due to overcrowding of fish and an excess of fish waste matter, on which bacteria feed and prosper. Cloudy water is similar, to some extent, to green water (which is algæ feeding on the same thing under the stimulus of light), and when the light is cut down bacteria take over. It is just another example of nature setting its own balance in the water.

Bacteria can be encouraged by excessive fish food, or by feeding a dry food which contains an ingredient the fish refuse to eat. But another cause is too few plants to absorb the waste matter or an insufficiency of light to stimulate them into the necessary action.

With an aquarium that is new, cloudiness is almost certain to be caused by sand that is not properly clean. In fact, a new aquarium is particularly prone to cloudy water until the plants get into action, and for this reason I advise you to leave a new aquarium without fish for about a week to give the plants a chance to do their work.

Another way to clear up cloudy water is to dissolve one-fifth grain by weight of permanganate of potash into each gallon of water. The fish or plants need not be removed as this is a weak solution and is harmless. Whilst this treatment will clear the water, the underlying cause must be cleared up, otherwise the condition will certainly reoccur.

If the water takes on a yellowish tinge, there is nothing for it but to change the water completely. As soon as your water shows the onset of decay, it is a serious business, and no time should be lost in putting it right. Delay may mean the loss of valued fish.

Oxygen

Oxygen is vital to all life, and in a limited volume, such as the aquarium, it is even more important to ensure that there are sufficient plants to maintain your fish in comfort. For unless you do so, the fish cannot do anything to help themselves.

Plants are the normal oxygenators, and under suitable conditions provide all that is necessary, but with overcrowded tanks it is necessary to aerate artificially. This also helps when you are breeding certain types of fish, and you can do it by installing a small air pump, electrically operated, which is quite inexpensive to buy. A small tube is carried from the pump to the bottom of the tank, and the end inserted into a porous stone, which diffuses the air into a thin stream of bubbles. One pump can, in fact, be used to serve several tanks.

Artificial aeration is particularly valuable at night when the plants fail to give off oxygen, and give off carbon dioxide instead. The bubbles forced into the tank do not actually became dissolved in the water themselves, though some of the air does, but the majority of oxygen comes from the surface of the water, which is circulated by the rising column of bubbles. It must be remembered that, as there is a limit to the amount of oxygen the water can hold, the greater the surface area the better.

It is not advisable to aerate continuously in this manner as the fish will become dependent upon it, and find some discomfort when moved to a tank with static water.

Warm water holds less oxygen than cold. Whilst water at a temperature of 50°F holds 7·8 parts per 1,000 by vol., water at 90°F holds only 5 parts. This shows how quickly the oxygen content decreases as the temperature increases.

Filters

Filters may be purchased ready for use made from Perspex, and for hygienic reasons it is better to use this type than to make your own from other materials which might contaminate the water.

The corner filter is simply a container into which a filtering medium—glass wool, charcoal, pebbles, and coarse sand, for instance—is packed. The water is then raised from the tank by means of the aeration pump, through a 'U' tube, and then poured back into the tank through the filter.

A filter of this type will remove much of the larger organic matter suspended in the water, and will usually clear up the condition of slightly cloudy water. You should clean the filter at least once a week if it is in continual use.

The biological filter is a bottom filter that can have certain advantages over the conventional types, but it must be used properly.

Without getting too technical, this type of filter employs bacteria to convert the aquarium waste into beneficial mineral salts. The equipment consists of perforated tubes buried in the gravel, usually in the shape of a rectangular framework, and a vertical air-lift tube. Air is

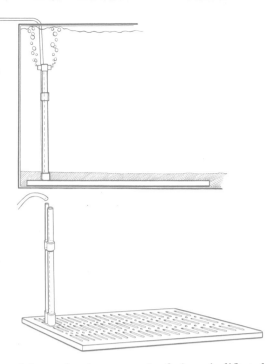

pumped into the lower end of the air-lift tube which causes the water contained in it to rise and overflow back into the tank. This action naturally tends to suck water in to replace the water expelled, and the result is that water passes *down* through the gravel, through the perforated tubes, and back into the tank, via the air-lift tube, and in so doing brings the organic waste material down between the grains of gravel. Bacteria, which are present on the surfaces of gravel grains, then convert this waste into salts which are useful to plant growth. During this process a certain amount of acid is formed which, if produced in excessive amounts, tends to reduce the size of the leaves of plants, and is also disliked by some species of fish.

The depth of sand is important, in theory the deeper the better, but consider 2 in. to be a minimum. Grain size also has an effect on the efficiency of under-gravel filtration, if the grains are too large, they accept more food than is required, and we have an unnecessarily high concentration of bacteria, and, of course, an attendant increase in acidity of the water. If the grains are too small, however, they will pack tightly together and this will prevent the bacteria doing the job.

Check occasionally to see if too much food is penetrating the sand by stirring the sand, if the top ½-in. layer is caked, you are allowing excessive food to reach the bacteria.

Filters are normally operated from small air pumps and employ the air-lift principle, but with the increased interest in marine aquaria, where filtration is more important, the range of filters has notably increased. Power filters, which suck the water from deep in the tank, pass it through the filter media, and return the water to the tank via a spray tube, can be obtained relatively cheaply. They are capable of filtering up to 60 gallons per hour, for both fresh and salt water.

The various filter manufacturers usually recommend the best combination of filter media, but these need not necessarily be adhered to strictly. Some aquarists do not like to use glasswool, for instance, but gravel, carbon, peat and the various proprietary media offer an adequate choice.

The disadvantage of glass fibre, or spun glass, is its tendency to break into fine splinters which find their way into the aquarium and are eaten by the fish, or stick in their gills causing inflamation.

There are many proprietary filter arrangements available, and whilst experienced aquarists may find them unnecessary items of equipment, they do help to keep the water clear and visually attractive, but they should not be considered a panacea for all water problems.

Metals

There are very few metals that can be used unreservedly in water. Lead is the best, and it can be used extensively, but unfortunately it is not rigid enough for some of the uses to which we would like to put it. Avoid brass, galvanised iron, and zinc, as they corrode and poison the water.

If your aquarium has a brass frame, the only part that can cause trouble is the top inside edge, the remainder of the frame is insulated by cement and glass. Cover this edge with cement or paint.

Iron will rust and, although it is not poisonous, drops of rusty water falling into the tank are not very desirable, so you should treat iron frames with cement or paint.

Nickel plating corrodes after a spell in water; so it should not be relied upon as a permanent protection.

Tap water

Most of us are compelled to fill our aquaria from the tap. Personally, I prefer to do so, rather than use pond water which may contain larvæ of dragon-flies, or water beetles.

Various districts have different quality water, and in this respect hard water is not good for plants or fish. Hard water can be improved by boiling, allowing to cool, and then drawing off from the top by using a piece of rubber tube as a siphon. The lower portion of the water should be thrown away.

Clean rain water can be used if you filter it through fine muslin and add two level teaspoons of sea salt to make up for any deficiency of minerals. The water may become cloudy when you add the salt, but it soon becomes clear.

Tap water is chlorinated to disinfect it. High concentrations of chlorine are harmful to fish and it is safer to let tap water stand for a few days before using it—the chlorine will then have disappeared into the atmosphere.

pH value

It is often an advantage, even a necessity, to be able to determine the condition of the aquarium water with regard to its alkalinity or acidity—this condition is determined by ascertaining its pH value.

Technically, pH is the logarithm of the reciprocal of the hydrogen ion concentration. Some knowledge of chemistry is necessary to fully appreciate the meaning of this. However, the technicalities need not concern us here—it is sufficient to know that it is a measure of acidity or alkalinity. The scale reproduced below shows the full range from 0 to 14; 0 is maximum acid, and 14 maximum alkaline, pH7 is neutral—neither one nor the other. Therefore, it can be seen that the higher the pH the more alkaline the water (above pH 7) and the lower the pH the more acid (below pH 7).

Extreme conditions will not concern us here as fish could not hope to live in them. Ranges between about pH 5 to pH 8 will cover all our needs.

The method of judging is done by colour comparison. As a guide the scale is reproduced below:

0 1 2 3 4 5 6 7 8 9 10 11 12 13 14

Acid ←————————Neutral————————→ Alkaline

For testing aquarium water there are various methods. One is to add one drop of 0.04 per cent bromthymol blue to 20 drops of aquarium water in a test tube, and by the colour it turns the condition can be judged. Green—neutral, blue—alkaline, yellow—acid; and the depth of colour indicates the degree of concentration.

You can buy a test set with small sealed test tubes filled with water, accurately coloured for comparison, and marked with the necessary reading.

Small books of indicator paper prepared for the aquarist, with a colour grading chart on the inside cover, are an inexpensive means of testing pH values.

To correct a deficiency of alkali, add salt, or sodium bicarbonate ($NaHCO_3$). Sea salt is best mixed with water before it is poured into the aquarium. This is better than table salt, as table

Xiphophorus hellerii
Xiphophorus hellerii
Hyphessobrycon innesi

34

salt usually has chemicals added to ensure free running.

Acid sodium phosphate (NaH_2PO_4) may be added to obtain a more acid condition. Always make a solution with water before stirring into your tank, and check the aquarium water afterwards to ensure that the correct condition has been attained.

The addition of acid sodium phosphate usually causes a thin film of precipitate to form on the water surface. This can be avoided if it is possible to boil the water first and then add potassium hydrogen tartrate ($KHC_4H_4O_6$) instead of acid sodium phosphate.

A final word of warning—do not drastically alter the pH value of any water containing fish. A quarter of a degree of the scale every twelve hours should be considered a maximum.

Water hardness

Water hardness has been included in this volume expressly for the benefit of the aquarist who enjoys experimenting with fish that are difficult to breed, and would like, at least to some extent, to be in a position to establish another water condition.

Water hardness need not be considered when breeding the easier fish, but is quite important when attempting to breed fish like the neon tetras, which prefer soft water. Water is said to be hard when soap refuses to lather readily in it and soft when it does. The actual cause of hardness is the impurities the water contains—these can be divided into three main groups, dissolved, suspended, and colloidal. Colloidal suspension is a state between true suspension and solution. Suspended matter and matter in colloidal suspension can usually be removed by filtration.

It is the presence of dissolved compounds of calcium and magnesium that is the major cause of water hardness. Some of these minerals are absorbed by the plant life, but exactly how much this would reduce the hardness of water in an aquarium is problematical.

The total hardness of a water includes both temporary and permanent hardness. The temporary hardness is due to the presence of calcium and magnesium bicarbonates, which can be removed by boiling the water. The permanent hardness cannot be removed so easily; it does not disappear with boiling. The cause is due to the presence of dissolved sulphates and chlorides of calcium and magnesium. As these are in solution, they cannot be removed by filtration, or by boiling.

Hyphessobrycon flammeus
Jordanella floridae
Copeina arnoldi
Hyphessobrycon innesi

Specific chemical treatment is often required which is beyond the average aquarist, but it is possible to reduce the permanent hardness by the addition of washing-soda (sodium carbonate, Na_2CO_3). This reacts with the calcium sulphate and forms a deposit of insoluble calcium carbonate, leaving sodium sulphate dissolved in the water.

All natural waters contain some impurities, even rain water which is the purest, therefore really soft water is undesirable and an unnatural element for our fish; the presence of some mineral salts is essential for both fish and plants.

Water hardness can be expressed in various ways, the modern trend is to use parts per million of calcium carbonate, but for convenience a conversion table is given on page .

Natural waters vary considerably. The composition of the ground over which the water flows after falling to earth as rain will determine most of the impurities it will contain, in addition to any it may have collected on the way down. Tap water also varies considerably with the district. The easiest way to obtain water of a definite hardness is to use distilled water (pure) and add tap water or sea salt until the desired hardness is obtained. This can be checked by using a standard soap

WATER HARDNESS— CONVERSION TABLE	Deg Clark		German deg	
	Parts/ 1,000,000	Grains/ gal	Parts/ 100,000	Parts/ 100,000
Parts/million as CaCo₃	1·00	0·07	0·10	0·056
Deg Clark Grains/gal as CaCo₃	14·3	1·00	1·43	0·80
Parts/100,000 as CaCo₃	10·0	0·70	1·00	0·56
German deg Parts/100,000 as CaO	17·8	1·24	1·78	1·00

Soft	Under 50 parts per million
Mod. Soft	Between 50–100 parts per million
Slightly Hard	Between 100–150 parts per million
Mod. Hard	Between 150–250 parts per million
Hard	Between 250–350 parts per million
Very Hard	350 upwards

solution. There are more accurate ways such as completely evaporating a given volume of water and accurately weighing the residue, but this method is obviously far too involved for the aquarist. To assess the hardness by the standard soap solution method, drops of liquid soap are added to a given quantity of water and by the number of drops required to obtain a permanent lather the hardness is ascertained.

If distilled water is difficult to obtain, clean rain water, filtered, and with a little sea salt added (about one level teaspoonful per gallon) is a good second best. The subject of water hardness cannot of course be dealt with fully in this volume, but most of the points affecting fish-keeping have been covered.

Cleaning

Aquaria should be cleaned once a week, especially if the main diet is dried food. Sediment collecting in the hollows and around the roots of plants can be removed with a siphon. This is simply a length of rubber hose, attached to a Perspex tube with one end shaped like a flattened funnel. The tube is filled with water and hung over the side of the tank into a container, and the other end held in the water near the sediment, which is sucked up by the rush of water.

There are several good sediment removers on the market which work either in conjunction with an aerating pump, or with a separate hand bulb. These have the advantage of removing the sediment without the water. Water and sediment are raised by air pressure up a tube with a 'U' bend at the top to which a muslin bag is attached. The water returns to the tank, but the sediment is collected in the bag.

You can remove green algæ on the glass with a razor blade scraper; these are specially made with a long handle for aquarium use. Snails will keep down most of the soft green algæ, but the hard, rusty brown type of algæ offers no attraction for them. Thread algæ, which, if left unhampered, will eventually choke the plants, can be removed with a rough piece of twig with the bark left on. Poke the stick among the algæ and twirl it, and you will be surprised how much thread algæ will be collected by this simple method.

Scum on the water surface is obnoxious because it hampers the oxygenation process and is likely to cause pollution. Scum is caused either by over-feeding (the uneaten food ferments), or by excessive lime in the water. You can remove scum by dragging a sheet of blotting paper across the water slowly from one end of the tank to the other, and then carefully lifting out the blotting paper. Newspaper can also be used to remove scum from the water surface. A sheet laid on the water, left for a few moments, and then carefully removed by peeling off from one end, will soon clean the surface. If not clean after one operation, repeat until the surface is to your liking.

Salt water

Without a doubt, marine aquaria should be filled with natural sea water obtained a few miles off shore, to avoid coastal pollution. This is not so easy to do for yourself, but it can be purchased from reliable dealers.

An economic substitute for large quantities of sea water can be made artificially (Louis C. Mandeville, *Water Life*, 4 Oct. 1938). The ingredients for L. C. Mandeville's formula are as the accompanying list.

The above formula has been included mainly for interest. A much simpler method is to purchase the necessary salts already compounded which only require the addition of water. Most of the large suppliers of aquaria and equipment will stock these salts.

When adding water to replace the loss caused by evaporation, always use distilled water. Remember that the mineral content of the water is not reduced by evaporation (see Change of Water).

Snails

Do not expect wonders from these scavengers. It is not reasonable to expect them to do all the dirty work, but they do help by eating any excess food, and in my opinion that alone warrants them a place in every aquarium.

Snails also keep down algæ by removing it from plants and the glass sides, and their paths are easily traced by a clean cut, but irregular, line through the algæ patch. They do not, however, completely clean the glass, though they make a good job of it.

My own favourite snails are the red ramshorns (*Planorbis corneus* var. *ruber*). Despite the fact they are European they have an exotic appearance, the best ones being bright red. Red ramshorns are also the largest of the species. They produce from 60 to 120 eggs in one season, which they lay in jelly masses containing 20 to 40 eggs. These hatch in 10 to 40 days, depending upon the temperature. If you particularly want to rear them, you should remove the eggs on the plant to an aquarium without any fish, as tropical fish will destroy the newly hatched youngsters. Pond snails, though not so spectacular as red ramshorns, perform their duties quite satisfactorily.

Generally snails tend to eat the plants, this is usually infuriating when a particularly favourite plant falls victim. There are exceptions to all rules and in this case the Malayan burrowing snail (*Thiara tuberculata*) is one.

This snail does not harm the plants, neither does it cover the leaves with eggs. It is quite distinctive and easily recognised by the shape of its shell which is an elongated cone, having about eight whorls. The shell has a ground colour varying between a lightish-brown and a grey-green, overmarked with brown spots which run more or less symmetrically along the length of the shell. As its name suggests, this snail has developed the

10 gal	Soft water		To these add:	
45½ oz	Common salt (sodium chloride)	⅕ oz	Potassium nitrate
1½ oz	Potassium chloride	10 g	Sod: acid phosphate
2 oz	Calcium chloride (dry)	5 g	Ferric chloride
8¾ oz	Magnesium chloride	½ gal	Natural sea water
11½ oz	Magnesium sulphate		
⅕ oz	Sodium bicarbonate		

habit of burying itself in the sand, leaving only a small portion of the shell tip above the surface. A fully grown specimen rarely exceeds $1\frac{1}{2}$ in. in length.

This slow-moving snail appears to exist solely on decaying animal and vegetable matter, or 'mulm'. Another interesting feature is the fact that the young are born alive. These tiny replicas are usually few in number and transparent, gaining their colour when about $\frac{1}{8}$ in. in length.

Netting

First obtain the correct shaped nets; rectangular ones are the best as the area of mouth is largest. They can be obtained in three useful sizes. You will probably need all three as it is hopeless to chase a fast moving fish with a net 2 in. × 1 in., and likewise it is ludicrous to net $\frac{1}{2}$-in. fry with a 6-in. net, as damage to the fish will be almost inevitable. Let patience guide you first, and experience later.

The best way to net your fish is to use two nets simultaneously—one net to catch, and the other to guide the fish. Very small, newly hatched fish should not be handled. They should be netted and brought to the surface still actually in water, and then removed in a large spoonful of water.

Fish tend to jump about when netted, and it is whilst doing this that injury is most likely to occur. They may even jump clean out of the net. The net should therefore be deep enough to form a bag that can be closed with the free hand.

A useful device for netting very small fish and fry, can be made by cutting the bottom away from a small rectangular net, and replacing it with oiled silk. The oiled silk retains a pocket of water to protect the little fellows.

Overcrowding

Overcrowding is a common fault. The beginner often keeps buying new specimens without making sure his aquarium will actually accommodate them. In a well-balanced aquarium, the number of plants should be roughly proportional to the number of fish. If overcrowding occurs, loss of some of the fish is inevitable.

Tropical fish can stand more overcrowding than cold-water fish. The latter require 24 sq. in. of surface per inch of fish, but tropicals need only about 8 sq. in. of surface area per fish. This density of fish should not be exceeded.

Change of water

It should not be necessary to change the water at all, providing the aquarium is balanced. I trust by now the word 'balance' has recurred a sufficient number of times under different headings for the would-be aquarist to realise that it is, in my view, the operative word throughout tropical fish maintenance. There are some conditions, however, when it is necessary to change the water wholly or partially. Some aquarists prefer to change 10 per cent of the water weekly. I have experimented up to 50 per cent, but found no definite benefit.

It must be remembered that when water evaporates from an aquarium, the minerals in the water remain behind and constant topping up with tap water increases the mineral content. Distilled water or clean rain water can be used without this happening.

Petty cruelties

It is thoughtless to suddenly switch on a bright electric light over the fish; they become startled and dart about in an agitated state.

Under the same category of petty cruelty is knocking on the glass to make a particular fish come out from behind a piece of rock or vegetation, or carelessly dropping the cover back on the top of the aquarium.

In fairness I do not believe that any of these things are generally done with the intention of frightening the fish, but that they are careless and thoughtless actions which can, and should, be avoided.

New arrivals

When fish are imported, there is always danger of an epidemic, but you can safeguard against this by quarantining the new fish for a few days before putting them into your stock aquarium. This is where your spare tank comes in useful.

New arrivals which you suspect should be put into a separate aquarium containing a solution of permanganate of potash to a strength of $\frac{1}{8}$ grain per gallon of water, and if you suspect white spot raise the temperature to 85° F. (See Diseases.) Fish obtained from sources known to be healthy need not be subjected to quarantine.

Never put new arrivals directly into their new home, but float the container in your aquarium water until the temperatures are the same, then tip them in. I advise you to do this because although some tropicals have a large temperature range, sudden changes are liable to cause disorders.

Bullies

I have noticed repeatedly that fish are bullies; they like to chase a smaller fish and seem to thoroughly enjoy the sport. Next day, perhaps the bully will be chased by another fish. It is therefore an advantage to try to keep fish of a similar size together. With a persistent bully, the only cure is to remove him to another tank in which he is not one of the largest.

Feeding

Quantity

The most important thing to remember about feeding is that overfeeding is one of the most common causes of pollution in aquaria. The appetite of fish is linked with environment, the warmer the natural conditions, the faster they breathe and grow (in fact, the whole process is speeded up) and the more they will want to eat.

Cold-water fish do not eat as much as tropical, under conditions which are normal to both. At a lower temperature than that to which they are accustomed, tropicals lose their appetite, but you can persuade them to regain this by raising the temperature.

The best method is to feed a little and often, and in this way the amount of food left uneaten is reduced to a minimum, though I realise it is impossible for the aquarist who is away all day at business to feed in this way. The next best way to feed is once in the morning and then in the evening. With dried foods the quantity should not exceed that which can be consumed within five minutes. If the fish are particularly ravenous a little more may be given. The ideal, however, is to keep the fish just hungry so that they are always foraging for food.

Feeding rings that float on the surface and contain the food in an area of say 4-in. square are quite useful in a tank with only one or two fish, as any uneaten food falls in the same place every time, and if you place a flat rock there it is easy to keep the tank clean. The disadvantage of ring-feeders may be seen when about twenty fish congregate under a ring, a great deal of pushing and shoving takes place, and the small fish have to rely on what is left over by their larger companions. It is not so important that live foods, such as tubifex worms, are consumed immediately, for they will live on in a healthy condition until they are eventually eaten.

During holiday periods, when it is necessary to be away for a week or more, you can give a heavier feed for a week prior to leaving, and if you drop the temperature to 70° F your fish will suffer little or no harm from a week without food.

If a longer period of absence is contemplated, and a friend has been asked to oblige, be sure to give him explicit instructions with regard to quantity. Frankly, a fortnight of wrong feeding can undo a lot of care, and I have found it best to provide the food in little packets of paper so that he only has to empty them into the tank.

Feeding marine tropicals

Feeding marine tropicals is more difficult than feeding freshwater species. Their natural foods are virtually unobtainable, and they do not generally take to dried foods, therefore, we must provide substitutes from the available live foods and meats. Small quantities of tubifex, daphnia, white worms, blood worms, shrimps, and bits of fish and meat will provide a reasonable variety.

Brine shrimps, *Artemia salina* (see page 41), are an excellent addition, but owing to their small size they have to be fed in large quantities to satisfy any large adult fish. Young guppies and mollies can be bred and fed as a live food. They have the advantage of being readily acclimatised to salt water. This is accomplished by adding, over a five-week period, one ounce of salt (Tidman's or sea-salt) to every gallon of water once a week. They are then ready to be put into the marine aquarium.

It is important to remember the susceptibility of salt-water aquaria to pollution. The fish should be fed daily, but any uneaten food should be removed if not consumed within a period of about 15 minutes.

Dry food

During the winter when live food is most difficult to obtain, a staple diet of dried food will have to be given.

Dried shrimp, obtainable in varying grades to suit various sizes of fish, will maintain fish in reasonably good health if occasional feeds of raw meat or live food are also given. Bemax mixed with a dry food is an excellent food which is rich in vitamins, but if given to smallish fish it should be rubbed through a fine mesh sieve.

There are numerous brands of prepared dried foods on the market, all of which claim to be the best. The ingredients that go to make these different foods are various, and it is almost impossible to judge the one most suitable for all occasions. My own method is to have a tin of all the well-known makes, and feed the fish from a different tin every day. This way the fish enjoy a maximum variety of diet.

Live foods

Live foods are an extremely valuable addition to diet, but they are not indispensable, except in the cases where fish are entirely carnivorous. Personally, I prefer to give the fish a balanced diet, when possible, of 50 per cent dry food and 50 per cent live food, the more varied the diet the better.

Daphnia

Daphnia are one of the best known live foods. They are found in almost every country in not too clean ponds, though it is not certain that every pond will contain daphnia. The most likely ponds

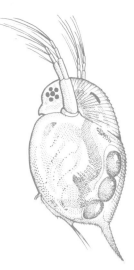

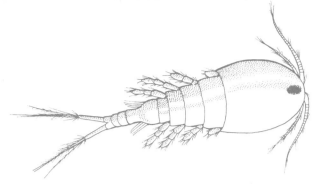

are those on farms into which a certain amount of manure finds its way. When you find a daphnia-producing pond, I advise you to guard your secret carefully, lest the news gets around and the pond is denuded.

How can you tell whether there are daphnia present? A cloud of daphnia seen in a pond looks like a million bugs all crawling, but getting nowhere. The colour of these little crustaceans varies from grey, green, to red. The red coloured are the most sought after, as they are believed to be the most nutritious.

Daphnia, like fish, need oxygen, and when an oxygen deficiency exists, they behave in the same way as fish—they rise to the surface. So on hot, humid days, you will see them just under the water's surface. As daphnia consume oxygen, a large quantity tipped into the aquarium at one time will cause discomfort to your fish.

Daphnia may be bought from most aquarium supply shops from the spring until autumn, or cultivated in the same way as cyclops. They can be graded to suit small fish, by straining in a large strainer similar to those used for straining baby foods, or an old wire mesh tea strainer.

Dried daphnia

Daphnia can also be obtained in a dried form. I see no reason why it should not be an excellent food in this form, but it is rather left to speculation as to how much of the goodness is destroyed in the drying process. Apart from that, dried daphnia has the advantage of being easily stored, and may be used when fresh daphnia is out of season.

Cyclops

Cyclops are very small crustaceans, usually found in ponds containing daphnia. They have the appearance of having only one central eye, and it is for this reason that they are named after the one-eyed giant in mythology.

These tiny crustaceans may be given to small fry fish just after the infusoria stage, but I think it

advisable to feed only the larger fish with them. A double sac containing eggs in some state of development will be found on the end of the female's body, and it is probably these that the fish find so tasty.

Cyclops are normally netted in the same way as daphnia, but if a few are introduced into a shallow dish of water containing infusoria, they will breed rapidly. An old porcelain sink with the drain plug sealed, and sunk into the garden is an ideal container.

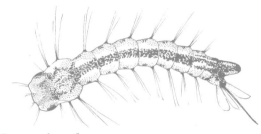

Mosquito larvae

Mosquito larvæ are another food you can collect from ponds. They can also be found in rain water butts, or even puddles. They hatch from the mosquito egg in a few days, and are easily recognised by their wriggly movement.

Their average length is about $\frac{1}{4}$ in., with a knob of a head on a worm-like body, with a Y-shaped end. They should not be given to fish under about $1\frac{1}{2}$ in. in length as the fish can easily choke themselves.

It is as well to point out that as daphnia and mosquito larvæ may be collected from foul pools, they should be rinsed before putting into your aquarium.

Brine shrimps (Artemia salina)

One of the most useful additions to an aquarist breeder's kit is a phial of dried brine shrimp eggs. These eggs are not in themselves a food, but when hatched out they provide an excellent early live food diet.

You can hatch the eggs in two-pound jam jars, in which a saline solution has been added. To make the solution, mix a tablespoon of salt with a pint of water thoroughly, shaking the container, then allow it to settle and strain through a piece of muslin to remove any sediment. Pour this water into the jar and sprinkle some eggs on the surface, and then stand the jar in an aquarium to keep at a temperature of 75°–80° F. This serves as an incubator. The eggs will hatch in 48 hours, leaving the little shrimps dancing about in the container.

To feed, strain the water through a pad made of several thicknesses of muslin, and rinse in the aquarium. You should only make up quantities sufficient for one feeding in each jar, as the collection of newly hatched shrimps can only be done by straining, unless the salt water is also poured into the tank, and I do not advise this when you are feeding young fry.

White worms (Enchytraeids)

White worm cultures are becoming the number one standby of modern fish-keeping for winter feeding. These small white worms, a relative of the earth worm, are about the same size as tubifex worms.

They are cultivated in a large tin containing damp soil, bulb fibre, or peat, and the nature of the soil should be such that it does not pack tightly, and you should mix plenty of leaf-mould with it. The original culture which you insert into the soil may be purchased from a fish dealer. Feed the culture, either by stirring in oatmeal (or drop it into holes in the soil made with a stick or pencil), bread wetted with milk, mashed potatoes, or Bemax. The worms will prosper and multiply. Do not overfeed, as it will turn the soil sour. If this should happen, however, start a new culture with some of the worms from the original one. Place the tin in a cool place, a cellar if available is ideal—the best temperature is around 60°F.

Before feeding white worms to your fish, thoroughly rinse them in water for about an hour to remove any dirt or parasites. A pair of tweezers is useful for separating worms that have congregated in a bunch.

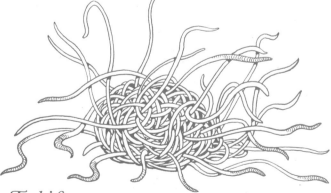

Tubifex worms

The main attraction of tubifex worms is the fact that they can be obtained all the year round, and they are also a substitute for daphnia. These thin rusty-red worms are relished by most fish, and when a bunch is dropped into the tank there is generally a rush to be the first customer.

Tubifex worms are usually found in localities such as small estuaries and flats of streams where there is plenty of mud and silt. The mud which contains the worms is lifted with a spade, put into a muslin bag, and washed in the stream to remove all but the worms. If tubifex are left in a shallow container, with about an inch of water, they will unite into a mass, and it is then easy to transfer them to your carrier jar.

Tubifex left uneaten in the tank separate from the bunch and scatter about singly, digging one end into the sand, and weaving as though in a strong breeze.

Do not store a large quantity in a jam jar as the weight of the top ones will kill the lower ones. Tubifex should be stored in a bucket or large tin into which a slow steady stream of water is flowing. The bunched worms can occasionally be separated with a stronger jet of water, which will wash out any dead and rotting ones.

Micro-worms (Anguillula silusiae)

These small worms are almost invisible without a microscope, and they only become visible to the naked eye when actually dropped into the water and then you can see them wriggling their way down to the bottom of the tank. They have now become an established live food for very young fish just out of the infusoria stage.

They are grown from a culture supplied by a dealer. You can make the stock in which the culture is to grow and multiply with soya flour, semolina, or oatmeal. Mix the oatmeal with water, $1\frac{1}{2}$ oz. to half a pint of water, cook, and then allow to cool. With soya flour or semolina, no cooking is necessary, just mix with water until it reaches the consistency of floppy paste. The culture is then put into the stock to cultivate. After a time the stock will deteriorate, but this need not worry you as a fresh stock can be made up and started off with a spoonful of the old one.

The micro-worm has an affinity to wet or damp wood, and it is this that allows it to be collected and fed without the stock also being introduced into the tank. Use a small paste pot with a metal lid to collect the worms. Punch twelve holes in the lid, so that twelve match sticks can be pushed into them with enough friction to hold them in position. Put a small quantity of the stock into the jar, roughly an $\frac{1}{8}$-in. depth will do, and push the match sticks down until they just touch the stock. Leave the micro-culture for a few hours in a warm room, after which enough worms will have found their way up the sticks to provide a meal. You will get the best results if the match sticks are thoroughly soaked in water before use.

Release the worms into the tank by immersing all the matches in the water with a brisk sideway movement which washes them off. If a large quantity of worms is needed, several paste pots can be made up. You can buy a set of six plastic containers set into a tray specially designed for this purpose from most dealers.

Earth worms

The lowly earth worm, so familiar to fish on the end of a hook, is generally acceptable to all fresh water fish. These worms are usually too large to be fed as collected, and will have to be chopped or sliced. An old pair of scissors does the job quite well, or you can use two steel plates with circular grooves like a coarse file. The worm is rubbed between the two plates which soon shreds it. Clean earth worms well before shredding.

Nottingham red worms are the best to use. Those that ooze a yellowish secretion should be thrown away. The fish will not eat them anyway.

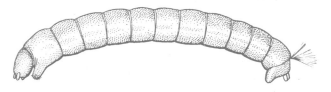

Blood worms

These small, deep red worms (usually about ½-in. long) can be fed to larger fish without chopping or shredding. Blood worms are found in daphnia ponds, and in many other watery places.

Blood worms are the larvæ of a midge, a species of *Chironomus*.

Freshwater shrimps (Gammarus pulex)

Freshwater shrimps are an excellent food, but as they are about ¾-in. in length they are only suitable for the larger fish. They are also useful scavengers, feeding on decaying animal and vegetable matter.

Infusoria

Infusoria is a loose term applied to organisms small enough to be fed to the very tiny young of most of the egg layers before they are old enough to be fed with sifted daphnia and brine shrimps.

To prepare infusoria, place squashed lettuce leaves in a quart of water, and leave out in the sun and air. The minute infusoria spores will settle on the water from the atmosphere and multiply on the products of the decaying lettuce. Chopped hay can also be used for preparing a culture, it is first boiled, then stood in a dark place.

It is advisable, while breeding, to start a new culture every four days to ensure a continuous supply. The water from a vase that has contained

chrysanthemums is also an excellent source of infusoria. Potatoes, banana skins, and crushed chrysanthemum leaves left in water for a few days, all provide a good infusion.

A small microscope is useful to see how rich the culture has become. Place a spot of water taken from the top of the jar on the glass slide, and examine. The spot should be teeming with life moving about like fine dust. Green water is actually a form of infusoria.

A few tropical infusoria snails (*Ampullaria paludosa*) put into a tank will soon result in a culture of infusoria, the partly digested droppings providing the necessary food. These snails feed on lettuce so ensure that there is always some available for them.

Excellent cultures may be made from dried lettuce leaves or duckweed. The leaves are thoroughly dried in an oven and stored in jars until required. This provides a way of making infusoria all the year round.

Rotifers

Rotifers are very small members of the animal kingdom, the largest being only just visible to the eye. They form an ideal early food for the fry of the larger species of fish. If put into an infusoria culture they will thrive.

Rotifers are found in ponds usually among the weeds, and one species, *Brachionus rubens*, may be found clinging to the body of daphnia. These are removed by washing the daphnia in a fine strainer under a jet of water. The rotifers then become detached and fall through, and the daphnia remain. When collecting rotifers a very fine net must be used; fine muslin will do.

Rotifers are divided into four classes—those that live in tubes, those that swim freely, those that creep like a leech, and those that progress by leaps—making altogether 700 species.

They are also referred to as 'wheel animalcules' because of the rapid movements of the cilia which surround the fore part of the body, giving the illusion of a rotating wheel. They reproduce themselves by eggs.

Glass worms (Chaoborus or Corethra larvae)

These worms, also known as ghost worms, are transparent and are not unlike the blood worms without the blood. They are about the same length, i.e. ½–¾ in.

They are found usually in ponds shaded by overhanging foliage and willows, where they can be seen lying in a parallel position a few inches below the surface. They suddenly disappear only to appear about a foot away, but facing the opposite direction. Their appearance is certainly ghost-like. When viewed in strong light they are practically invisible. The main advantage of the glass worms is that they are procurable during the winter months. They swim about in the water in search of food which can be anything from daphnia to rotifers.

They are caught in much the same manner as daphnia by sweeping the net through the water; this must be done steadily and swiftly. When captured they appear like a mass of jelly in the net end.

It is not every pond that will yield glass worms, but when they are found they are usually in great numbers. They lend themselves very well to storage. If more than can be used immediately are captured, the remainder can be stored in a small aquarium. Overcrowding seems to have little or no effect on them.

Despite their name these creatures are not worms, but are in fact larvæ of the plumed gnats.

Gentles

Gentles can be fed only to the larger fish. They are pale grubs, about ½-in. long and they are actually larval flies, particularly of the blow fly.

Gentles are much used by coarse fishermen, and can usually be purchased from suppliers of fishing tackle.

Food varieties

In an effort to provide a varied diet, the aquarist should not forget that meat scrapings (from lean meat only), dried yolk and white of eggs, and shredded boiled fish are all available from the household pantry, but remember again, *do not overfeed*.

Conditioning

Healthy fish are far more likely to spawn and give a higher percentage of fertilised eggs than those in indifferent condition. It is for this reason that all fish intended for breeding should undergo a period of condition feeding before any attempt at spawning.

Apart from ensuring that they have ample space, the best way to do this is by frequent meals of live foods (varied as much as possible).

Raw, finely lacerated meat, liver, fish, shrimp, crab, and lobster, can be hung on a piece of cotton into the tank, where it will be nuzzled and slowly torn to pieces. If not completely gone within an hour it is best to remove it.

Feeding young fish

When feeding flour-size dry food to fry, it should never be sprinkled on the water surface, as much of it will remain uneaten and decay. Also food fed in this way is too large for some of the smaller fry.

The best method is to make a stiff paste by the addition of a little water, then put the paste into a small muslin bag. To feed: screw the bag so that it squeezes the paste into a ball and then dip it into your aquarium containing the fry. The food will then come away from the bag in a fine cloud. It is also easier to control the quantity of food given by this method.

The following table is a quick guide to fry feed:

MENU No. 1. *Small Fry (Anabantids)*

1st Stage	2nd Stage	3rd Stage	4th Stage	5th Stage
Green water	Infusoria	Infusoria	Brine shrimp	Larger daphnia
Flour-size dry food		Micro-worms	Screened daphnia	Small dry food
		Rotifers	Chopped white worm	

MENU No. 2. *Medium Fry (Barbs, Characins)*

1st Stage	2nd Stage	3rd Stage	4th Stage	5th Stage
Flour-size dry food	Fine dry food	Brine shrimp	Larger dry food	Adult daphnia
Infusoria, Egg yolk, hard boiled and mixed with water	Fine grated shrimp Rotifers	Sifted daphnia Micro-worms	Chopped white worm Med. daphnia	Med. dry food

MENU No. 3. *Large Fry (Livebearers, Cichlids)*

1st Stage	2nd Stage	3rd Stage	4th Stage	5th Stage
Brine shrimp	Med. daphnia	Fine dry food	Adult daphnia	Larger dry food
Sifted daphnia		Chopped white worm		Chopped tubifex
Flour-size dry food				
Micro-worm				
Rotifers				

Diseases

It is obviously better to adopt the principle that 'prevention is better than a cure', when dealing with such a difficult subject as fish. Cleanliness, careful feeding, and attention to detail when introducing new plants and specimens will take care in advance of the majority of health problems. However, things go wrong in the best of circles, and when they do, take immediate remedial actions, but do take the time to diagnose the trouble, and always handle the fish carefully. If you have to take it out of its element, do so for the shortest possible time.

The treatments recommended are intended to give the aquarist an opportunity to cure fish that have some malady, but it is not an area where guaranteed results can be assumed.

Whenever possible, always endeavour to segregate fish under treatment into a hospital tank, to avoid infecting other healthy fish, and to avoid exterminating the contents of an otherwise healthy aquarium by accidental wrong treatments.

Segregation and feeding with live foods, will help to improve most sick fish.

Argulus (fish louse)

The fish louse is a free swimming crustacean that attaches itself to the fish in much the same manner as the anchor worm (page 47), and the treatment is the same. The disease can be recognised as greyish patches, usually round, attached to the skin of the fish, mainly around the belly, gills, and areas near the throat.

An alternative method of treatment is to treat the aquarium with potassium permanganate, $\frac{1}{3}$ grain to each gallon of water. Repeat as necessary every 8 to 10 days. No harm will come to the plants or fish.

Branchiitis (inflamation of the gills)

When the gills become inflamed and swollen, it is a sign that the fish is suffering from branchiitis. This disorder may be accompanied with white patches on the body and a general listlessness.

The cause is lack of available oxygen in the water, which is, in fact, asphyxiating the fish, this causes the gills to become inflamed due to being overworked.

The fish should be transferred to the hospital tank, in which the water level has been reduced to about 6 in. The water should be aerated, and the fish fed with small quantities of live food. The condition should clear up within 10 days.

Constipation

Occasionally a fish becomes constipated, or is subject to a form of stoppage in the intestines. The fish becomes generally 'out of sorts' sometimes refuses to eat, becomes thin and swims with fins closed. In this case, the fish should be put into a small aquarium by itself and Epsom Salts added to the water—half a teaspoonful to each gallon of water. If the cause of the illness is in fact constipation and this treatment is effective, the fish should pass heavy excreta. Halibut oil soaked into a small bread pill can also be tried.

Convalesce the fish by changing the aquarium water and feeding live foods for a few days. If this treatment should fail to cure the fish, it tends to indicate that the trouble may be due to internal growths or internal parasitic worms, in which case it would be kind to destroy the fish.

Costiasis

Costiasis is a disease that is nearly always fatal. By the time it can be diagnosed it is too late for treatment, and the fish is best destroyed to avoid spreading the infection among the other fish.

Costiasis is recognised by a reddish streak, not unlike a burn mark, spreading along the side of the fish from the tail towards the head. This streak causes all the mucus to disappear, and the scales to appear rough and inflamed.

Cyclochaetiasis (fin rot)

This disease usually affects the tips of the fins and tail first. It gives them a frayed and split appearance, as if they had been torn in combat. If allowed to continue in this condition the fish will surely die. It may be, of course, that a fish has nibbled the fins, but it is better to be safe than sorry, and in cases where treatment is necessary the following should be observed.

The rotting process is indicative of poor health. A conditioning diet of daphnia and chopped earthworms will help to put the fish on the road to recovery. The affected parts of the fins must be removed. This is quite easily done by holding the fish in a wet net and using a pair of sharp scissors, paint the stump with Friars Balsam afterwards.

Bath the fish in water to which 10 drops of $2\frac{1}{2}$ per cent solution of mercurochrome per gallon has been added. The fish should be left for a period of 20 minutes, but remove it sooner if it shows signs of distress.

A simpler method is to immerse the affected part in a solution consisting of one part water and one part peroxide of hydrogen (20 vols). This treatment should be carried out twice daily.

Dropsy

With dropsy, the fish take on a bloated appearance, so much so that it looks as if it will burst at any moment; the scales stand out from the body, and sometimes even the eyes will bulge.

A fish will suddenly develop dropsy for no apparent reason, but luckily it is never an epidemic, and after removal of the sick one, no other precautions are necessary to safeguard the others.

At the time of writing there is no known cure, and the disease usually proves fatal within three weeks. You can therefore save the fish some discomfort by destroying it immediately the symptoms develop.

Exophthalmia (pop-eye)

Pop-eye is caused by a haemorrhage produced by gas in the capillaries of the eye socket, and can affect either one or both eyes.

The treatment is to give a salt bath, as described for fungus (page 47), for a 36-hour period, then carefully bathe the eyes with a 5 per cent solution of Argyrol which is a mild silver proteinate.

Another method of treatment consists of a special bath consisting of one drop of ammonia to every gallon of water. The temperature of the bath should be increased to about 80° F and the fish left in the solution for about three hours. After this period, gradually reduce the ammonia content by adding new water until it is back to normal. The fish can then be returned to the original tank.

Frayed fins

Most fish at some time or another will have their fins bitten away by a fish called by aquarists 'a fin nibbler'. Many species of fish will, at odd times, develop this annoying habit.

The fins become frayed and jagged, but if the fish is removed away from any further attacks, the condition will soon right itself. However, if you feel some action should be taken, a salt bath will do no harm.

Ichthyophthirius (white spot)

Ichthyophthirius is the name of the parasitical organism responsible for this disease, which is easily recognised by a rash of white spots covering the body and fins. The spots are about the size of a pin head, and are caused by the parasite burrowing just below the skin and setting up an irritation. The first sign you may get of white spot is that your fish dart about among the plants or flick themselves against the rocks to ease the irritation, and the barometer of health, the fins, will be laid flat, not erect as with healthy fish.

If white spot is not checked at this stage, the spots multiply rapidly until they cover the whole body and fins in a film of fungus, which soon results in death.

The main cause of the trouble is a chill brought on by a sudden change in temperature. This change need not necessarily be of a low temperature, a sudden drop from 80° to 74° F is quite sufficient. Yet another cause is the introduction into your tank of a new specimen which has the disease.

The first step in the cure is to raise the temperature to 85°F and to keep it there for several days. You should do this irrespective of any treatment to follow.

The parasites develop on the fish until they reach their maximum size, usually in two or three days. Then they drop off on to the bottom of the tank, multiply several hundred times, and are then ready to start all over again. When the parasites drop off the fish, remove the fish to a sterilised tank (also at 85°F). If your fish have no sign of the white spot after about ten days you can consider them cured. Thoroughly sterilise the old tank before using it again.

Another method of curing white spot is to add three drops per gallon of 2 per cent mercurochrome to the infected tank, mixing the mercurochrome with a small quantity of water first. After a week, draw off half the volume of water, and replace with clear water. Some aquarists complain of loss of fish after this treatment from mercury poisoning, but I can only assume they use too strong a solution, for I have never lost a single fish with this treatment.

Another method is to use 2 drops of 5 per cent aqueous solution of methylene blue per gallon of water in conjunction with a temperature of 85°F, but this stains the sand and is not good for plants.

The modern treatment is to add 2 to 3 grains of quinine sulphate or quinine hydrochloride per gallon to the affected tank. Mix first with water and slowly stir into your aquarium, which should be kept dark during this treatment. This cure is, in my opinion, the most effective because it does not discolour the water, or harm the fish or plants.

Proprietary brands of white spot cures are quite effective, but as most of these are affected by light, make sure they are supplied in dark-coloured bottles.

Itch

Itch must not be confused with flukes or *Ichthyophthirius*, although the fish does dart about obviously suffering from some irritation. The actual cause is a microscopic organism in the water set up through an excess of uneaten food, and excretions being allowed to remain in the tank.

To cure, add $\frac{1}{8}$ grain of permanganate of potash per gallon of water to the aquarium; it will not be necessary to remove any fish or plants. Leave for two or three hours, then remove any settlings in the bottom of the tank with a siphon, emptying the aquarium by a half. Make up the deficiency with clear seasoned water. The slight shade of pink discoloration remaining will eventually clear.

Indigestion

Indigestion is usually caused by wrongful feeding such as excessive feeding of dried food, or it can be caused by constipation. Indigestion can be recognised by a swollen belly, air bubbles in the faeces, and general sluggishness. It is not a serious complaint, but needs speedy action, or it may lead to a more serious condition.

The treatment is the same as for constipation.

Lernaea (anchor worm)

Anchor worms are parasitic, free swimming crustaceans that attach themselves to fish and feed on their blood.

The treatment consists of removing the fish, and touching the anchor worms with a camel hair pencil brush dipped in paraffin oil, or turpentine, and then removing the offender with a small pair of tweezers.

0.1 per cent solution of potassium permanganate can be used instead of paraffin oil.

Melanosis (black fungus)

Fish suffering from this disease exhibit dark furry patches on the body. It is caused by disorders of the blood and general debility.

The treatment is the same as for fungus, but the affected parts can also be painted with a solution of one part water to one part peroxide of hydrogen (20 vols) occasionally.

Mouth fungus

Mouth fungus is an odious disease, and is, luckily, rather rare. When one fish has it, it can contaminate all the fish in the same tank, as it is highly contagious. The disease becomes apparent when a cottony fluff appears around the lip and mouth, which soon gets into the mouth and eats the jaws away.

Owing to the highly contagious nature of the disease, instant action is called for. Unfortunately, very little is known about the disease, and no treatment has been devised to treat the fish *en masse*. Dab the lips with cotton wool soaked in peroxide of hydrogen (20 vols) straight from the bottle, or mentholate. Handle the fish carefully, hold it in an absorbent soft linen thoroughly soaked in water, or in a wet net. Salt baths can also be tried, but the actual effect of the salt has not yet been proved. At least it has no harmful effect.

Fish most likely to develop this type of fungus are those which have suffered bruised lips whilst being transported.

Oodinium (velvet)

This disease can be recognised by a yellow-brown film which starts near the dorsal fin, and, if left unchecked, it will spread all over the body in a velvet-like film.

To treat, dissolve one tablet of Acriflavine (0.46 grain, obtainable from chemists) in eighty drops of hot water, then add five drops of this solution to every gallon of water to be treated.

During this treatment the aquarium should be kept dark, and artificially aerated. Repeat treatment after five days.

Saprolegnia (fungus)

Fungus is the white slimy coating that fish develop following an attack of *Ichthyophthirius*, which has not been cured. It can also develop independently, but is rather rare in tropicals. Bruises, chills, wrongful feeding, attacks by other fish, and dirty aquariums are all possible causes of fungus.

The fish should be put into a container of water devoid of vegetation, containing two level teaspoons of salt per gallon of water. Sea salt is better than common salt. If after 24 hours no improvement is seen, add two more teaspoons of salt, and, if by the third day no change is noticed, add another teaspoon.

When the fish is cured, do not put it straight back into its normal tank without first adding fresh water gradually, over a period of two days, to lower the salt content. This ensures that it is not subjected to a drastic change of water which might have an adverse effect on a fish just recovering from an illness.

Shimmies

Shimmies is more a sympton than a disease, it is the outward sign that all is not as it should be. The fish usually stops in one position waving its body from side to side like a hula dancer, the movement being slow and constant.

Fish with *Ichthyophthirius* are liable to act in this manner; indigestion, chills, etc. are other possible causes.

Completely changing the water often cures this trouble. It is believed that a micro-organism in the water of a none too clean tank can bring on this condition. If a change of water fails, increase the temperature to a steady 80°F and feed sparingly.

Swim bladder

The swim bladder is the organ of depth control, and acts similarly to the ballast tanks of a submarine, but instead of being filled with water, a gas developed in the fish is the medium of altering buoyancy.

It will be appreciated that in the delicately balanced bladder of a fish, the gas pressure must be exactly correct, if it is to swim freely wherever it desires. If there is too little gas it will sink, and with too much it stays on the surface. Gases which form internally through other causes, such as indigestion, sometimes have a temporary effect, but any prolonged upset will certainly be a defective swim bladder, which unfortunately is usually incurable.

Trematodes (flukes)

Parasitic organisms called *Gyrodactylus* and *Dactylogyrus* are the cause of flukes, which are highly contagious. They lodge in the gills and under the skin causing the fish to swim about in a wild and jerky manner, suddenly coming to a stop with every appearance of exhaustion.

Again there are various treatments for this illness, but the most successful one, in my experience, is the formaldehyde bath. You make up a bath of clear water, to which you add 20 drops per gallon of formaldehyde, then immerse the fish for between 5 to 8 minutes, or until it shows signs of discomfort or exhaustion. The treatment should be repeated in two days, after which the fish should be cured.

Another effective treatment is to place the fish in a bath made up of one part of (20 vols) hydrogen peroxide to five-hundred parts of water. The fish should be left in this solution for several hours.

When it is necessary to treat the majority of fish in an established aquarium, make a solution by dissolving 15 grains of methylene blue in $3\frac{1}{2}$ fluid ounces of water. This solution is then added to the aquarium in the proportion of one or two cubic centimetres to every gallon of water. Naturally the water in the aquarium will turn very blue, but within a few days it will regain its normal clarity. It is not necessary to change the water, or to repeat the treatment.

Another method is to immerse the affected fish in a bath containing one drop of glacial acetic acid to each ounce of water. Repeat treatment after 48 hours.

Tuberculosis (wasting)

Every now and again a fish will, for no apparent reason, virtually waste away; become hollow bellied, listless, and lie around on rocks or on the sandy bottom in a most dejected manner. The contributing factors to this malady are underfeeding, an unsatisfactory diet, overcrowding, or water which has been too warm or too cold over a period.

Fish suffering from wasting seldom survive. I have tried many treatments without any one single case of real success. The only treatment to try is a general conditioning. Allow plenty of room for movement, feed live food (beef scraped with a knife is also usually an acceptable tit-bit), chopped earthworm or daphnia.

Fish do eventually die of old age, in which case they naturally waste away.

Wounds

Sores, unless treated early, are liable to develop into fungus. Fish can wound themselves by knocking against sharp pieces of rock or stones when in a panic, or they can be nipped by a larger specimen.

The best treatment is to dab the wounds with a small piece of cotton wool soaked in 2 per cent mercurochrome, or by pouring a strong solution of permanganate of potash directly into the wound, and then washing off with fresh water. The fish obviously needs to be netted before either of the above treatments can be carried out. Remember to handle the fish carefully and to protect the gills by covering them lightly with a piece of soft material *soaked* in water.

Antibiotics

At the time of writing this book the use of antibiotics as a cure for fish diseases has not been fully explored and, although serious-minded aquarists are experimenting, no complete or specific information can be included. In America these drugs are somewhat easier to obtain by the public at large, so it is not surprising to find the Americans use them more than we do here in Britain.

An antibiotic is a chemical substance produced by one organism that is detrimental or lethal to another. The most publicised, at least in Britain, is penicillin. Antibiotics are not new. Scientists have known of their existence for the last fifty years, during which period they have been used spasmodically for the treatment of infections to mammals. The most notable of these antibiotics was pyocyanase, an antibacterial substance produced by the microbe of blue pus, but it was the discovery of penicillin by Sir Alexander Fleming that really put these drugs in the forefront. The chemical product, or antibiotic, is produced primarily in large quantities by fungi and bacteria.

Many of the diseases to which tropical fish are subject are caused by fungi, bacteria, viruses, parasites, etc., and whilst it is practically impossible for the average aquarist to diagnose these diseases without the necessary scientific training, it is reasonable to assume that most of them are caused by the invasion of the system by disease-producing bacteria or micro-organisms, and therefore can be experimented upon with antibiotics. It must be realised that fish treated with these types of drug should not be left in contact with them any longer than is necessary. Fish can be treated by adding the drug to the water or, if necessary, the drug may be applied directly to the affected part.

It would be advisable in these early stages to restrict the use of antibiotics to diseases not easily diagnosed, or not curable by any other known method.

Aureomycin is one of the newer drugs and may be tried as a cure for mouth fungus. The suggested concentration is about 50 milligrammes to a gallon of water. Aureomycin is practically insoluble in water of an acid nature and readily soluble in alkaline. Should the water in which you wish to treat your fish be of an acid nature, the drug can be given by mixing with a prepared food.

Chloromycetin has an action similar to aureomycin, but probably has a better reaction in acid water. Other drugs of an antibiotic nature are neomycin, polymyxin, tyrothricin, terramycin, bacitracin, and streptomycin.

Enemies

Generally speaking, the likelihood of fish enemies in the aquarium can almost be disregarded, but there is a possibility of accidentally introducing them with live foods.

Dragon-fly larva

It is possible when collecting daphnia to include a few dragon-fly larvæ in the net. Unfortunately, any strainer that lets daphnia through will also pass the small larvæ.

There are various species, the ringed club dragon-fly (*Cordulegaster annulatus*) and the giant dragon-fly (*Aeschna grandis*), are two of the best known, but they can all be considered under one heading. Their method of attack is to lie and wait

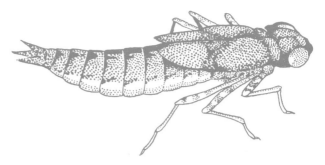

until a fish comes within striking distance, then quickly extend the mask which fastens tightly on to the fish. The mask is the organ carrying the mouth and pincers which can be thrust forward at will. The pincers hold the victim whilst the fish is eaten into. Propulsion is by means of a stream of water violently squirted from the body, although some species get along by wriggling the tail like an oar.

The life of these larvæ lasts about a year. The larva then becomes like a squat beetle, at which stage it leaves the water to become a dragon-fly.

They are particularly dangerous to young fry, and the only prevention is to keep a close scrutiny on live foods.

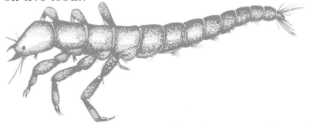

Dystiscus marginalis (water tiger)

The water tiger is far more dangerous than the dragon-fly larva. It is the larval form of the large cruel water beetle (*Dytiscus*), and much more likely to be included with live food as it is a free swimmer.

There are several species, but from the aquarist's viewpoint the following holds true of them all. Water tiger larvæ are hard to distinguish when small and mixed with daphnia.

Their method of attack is different from the dragon-fly larvæ, which are content to lie in wait. The water tiger will actually chase a victim and sink its two hollow mandibles into it, through which it sucks sufficient blood to kill. It then goes off after another victim.

The maximum size is 2 in., and at that stage they are easy to detect, but you should never allow them to reach such maturity in the aquarium. When they are only $\frac{1}{4}$ in. in length they can mingle with young fry, and will eventually kill them all unless they are discovered.

The only real precaution is vigilance. Fortunately, some large fish will eat them, especially cichlids.

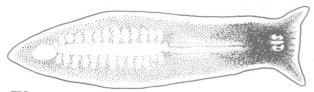

Flat worm

Flat worms are usually between $\frac{1}{8}$ to $\frac{3}{16}$-in. long, and coloured a pale grey, similar to the body of a garden snail. They can be seen crawling on the glass of the aquarium. Flat worms are not enemies in the true sense of the word, but they are undesirable. They feed on microscopic organisms, and if placed in clear water will soon perish through lack of food. They can be trapped on a piece of raw meat. You suspend the meat by a piece of cotton in the aquarium. The meat should be guarded to prevent the fish eating it. If you start the treatment in the evening you will find next morning that there are flat worms crawling over the meat, which you can then remove. Continue this treatment until the trouble is cleared up.

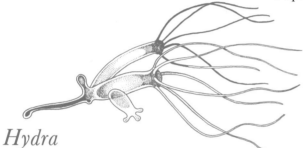

Hydra

The hydra is only dangerous to very small fish. It is a low form of life, a polyp, that devours fish up to about $\frac{3}{16}$-in. long, and also daphnia.

It has from three to seven tentacles spreading from the mouth in a star-like formation, to which the thin elongated body is attached. The actual shape is not the same in all specimens. They differ widely, making it almost impossible to describe them without going into volumes of detail.

It attacks by waiting for a fish or daphnia to pass near enough to be caught by the tentacles. It is then drawn into the mouth to be digested— undigested portions being returned through the mouth. It is not uncommon for a single hydra to have daphnia held by each tentacle waiting their turn to be devoured.

They multiply themselves by budding and division, and given good conditions propagation is rapid.

You can get rid of this pest by removing all your fish and bringing the temperature of the water up to 105°F. This is rather an inconvenient method,

and you may prefer to add one teaspoonful of household ammonia to every five gallons of water. Allow this to stand for two hours after which a complete change of water must be made in the aquarium. The ammonia will not harm the plants, but fish must be removed.

Leeches

Again we have a pest that is not really an enemy. On rare occasions leeches may attach themselves to fish, but this is the exception rather than the rule.

There are many species of leeches, far too many to enumerate here, but anything that crawls with a flattish body can be assumed to be a leech. Some species have a sucking disc at each end which enables them to crawl like a caterpillar, looping and extending the body.

They are very hardy, being able to withstand the action of chemicals to a greater extent than the plants, so it will be obvious that treatment chemically is not suitable. Raw meat suspended in the aquarium as for flat worms is about the most effective method.

Limnaea (great pond snail)

The great pond snail, whilst being a general feeder, has a strong leaning towards animal matter, and if put into a tank containing hydra will soon eliminate them. It is quite safe to put these snails in an aquarium containing young fry.

The gouramis are some of the few fish that will eat hydra. They may not, however, consume all of them.

Thread worm

There are many different kinds of thread worms. They are recognised as hair-like creatures, wriggling their way about the tank with eel-like motions of the body.

They need not be considered a danger, but they are an unpleasant sight to the conscientious aquarist who takes a pride in his tanks. They can be eliminated by the same treatment as specified for cleaning plants.

Water beetles

Nearly all water beetles are carnivorous, and it is extremely unlikely that they will find their way into the aquarium if reasonable care is taken to keep them out. Any that slip in should be removed immediately.

Fish

Classification

It is not necessary to understand or study fish classification to keep fish, but considerable enjoyment can be achieved if a little time is spent on gaining a working knowledge of the subject.

The total number of species in the world can only be estimated roughly. The British Museum (Natural History) gives an approximation of 30,000, all of which, as far as possible, are catalogued into various groups depending upon the internal and external salient features of the differences. From this vast number of species it will be obvious that a detailed account would be impossible in this volume. It is possible, however, to show broadly how ichthyologists classify fish, and introduce you to a subject which you can, if you desire, pursue on your own.

First it is necessary to know the names of the external features of the fish, for this is the only way amateur ichthyologists have of recognising the group to which the fish belongs.

Most fish have seven fins, four of which are paired. The first pair, those nearest the gill cover, are the pectoral or breast fins, and correspond to hands. The second pair are the ventral or pelvic fins, situated on the underside just below or behind the pectoral fins, and these correspond to legs. Between the tail and ventral fins is the anal fin, and this is situated *behind* the ventrals. Next comes the tail or caudal, which is used by most fish as a propulsion unit. The fin on the top part of the body is the dorsal, and this may be either short and upright, broad and extending to the length of the back, or even in two separate halves. Some species have an extra fin—the adipose, which is situated on the back between the dorsal and the caudal.

The fins are composed of a fine membrane, stiffened and supported by fin rays which are jointed and spread as they near the edge of the fin.

In some fish, notably the cichlids, the dorsal and anal fins have the foremost rays sharp and unjointed. These bony rays are known as spiny, and the remaining part as soft, and the fins are referred to as spiny and soft dorsal, etc.

It is the formation and position of the fins, plus other differences, mostly of an internal nature, that control the whole system of classification.

The main group of fish that interest us will be Teleostei or bony fish, for most of the aquarium fish are of this class.

The class is sub-divided into orders, orders into families, families into genera, genera into species. This at first reading may seem a little complicated, but for a clearer explanation imagine an army division as the class, which is broken down into regiments and companies, until finally we have the soldier, who represents the species.

Very old fish of a bygone age, of which only fossils remain, are placed first, and the others follow on in order, according to their development.

The super-order Ostariophysi, order Cypriniformes, is the order in which Characins, carps and

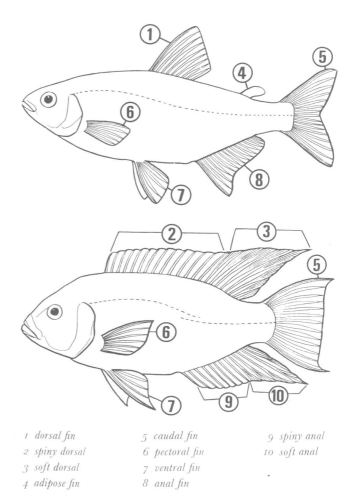

1 dorsal fin	*5 caudal fin*	*9 spiny anal*
2 spiny dorsal	*6 pectoral fin*	*10 soft anal*
3 soft dorsal	*7 ventral fin*	
4 adipose fin	*8 anal fin*	

minnows, and hatchet fish are placed.

The super-order Atherinomorpha, order Atheriniformes, is the order in which the tooth carps, both viviparous and oviparous, are placed together with the silversides.

The super-order Ostariophysi, order Siluriformes, is the order in which the catfish are placed.

The super-order Acanthopterygii, order Perciformes, is the order in which the Cichlids, scats and Nandids are placed.

To use all the five terms continuously would prove rather cumbersome, so for all general purposes the last two are enough. Genus being placed before species.

Sometimes it is necessary to subdivide the species into what is called a variety, and this is abbreviated to 'var.'. For instance, *Platypœcilus maculatus* var. *ruber*. Variety is only used in this sense. When the word species is used after the genus, instead of the name, it means the genus is known but the species is not. For instance, *Barbus species*. (Note: plural of species is species, and of genus is genera.)

To save needless repetition, the ichthyologist uses the abbreviation of the first letter of a genus, instead of the whole word, providing it has been quoted in full previously. *Lebistes reticulatus* would be repeated *L. reticulatus*.

The following is a typical example of classification:

Class	Teleostei
Super-order	Ostariophysi
Sub-order	Characoidei
Family	Characidae
Genus	*Aphyocharax*
Species	*rubripinnis*

The *Aphyocharax rubripinnis* is commonly called a bloodfin.

The classification used in the Fish Gallery of the British Natural History Museum is that proposed by Dr. C. Tate Regan, F.R.S., and is explained in articles by him on 'Fishes', 'Selachians', etc. in the Fourteenth Edition of the Encyclopædia Britannica (1929).

A copy of the 'Illustrated Guide to the Fish Gallery', obtainable from the Natural History Museum, is a welcome addition to the library of those wishing to pursue this subject.

The super-orders and orders preceding each section on fish have been adopted from the *Bulletin of the American Natural History Museum*, 'Provisional Outline Classification of the Teleostean Fishes' by Greenwood, Rosen, Wertzman and Myers, published December 1966. This work was primarily concerned with family classification, therefore the scientific names of fish used have not been altered from those in current usage.

Breeding
Live-bearing tooth carps (viviparous)

The fact that fish can bring forth their young alive has always been a source of amazement to the uninformed. This startling fact is probably responsible for more people taking up the hobby than any other factor. Whilst it is true that the young are born alive, they are not born quite in the same sense as mammals.

The egg is the medium used by all live-bearing animals to pass on life and perpetuate the species. In the case of mammals the fertilised egg attaches itself to part of the female where it develops, drawing sustenance from her bloodstream, until it is ready to enter the world. The period of gestation is consistent with every species.

But with live-bearing fish this is not so. The eggs are situated in the egg duct where they are fertilised. Upon hatching, the young are not immediately delivered, but remain until they reach a stage of development, equivalent to the young of egg-laying fishes that have absorbed their yolk-sacs, and become free swimming. The young are folded once inside the mother, and are delivered singly. They soon straighten themselves and swim to any plant or rock that offers them refuge. When first seen in the aquarium they are about a $\frac{1}{4}$-in. long, which is much larger than those of the majority of species that lay eggs to be developed externally. Their big advantage is naturally the protection of their mother's body until they are equipped to meet the outside world.

Unlike mammals, the period between fertilisation and birth is not standard, and is considerably influenced by temperature. As an average, this period is between four and five weeks at a temperature of 75°F. When the temperature is dropped the period increases considerably. At 68°F it may take as long as 11 weeks before delivery. A temperature in the region of 80°F induces rapid incubation of the eggs, and tends to make more robust fry.

Sexing is no problem, even to the inexperienced eye, as the novice can learn to distinguish the difference in a few minutes. At birth, and for a few weeks afterwards, it is impossible to sex, but as the male nears maturity the anal fin becomes more pointed and lengthens into a rod-like projection in no way resembling a fin—this is called the gonopodium. The gonopodium is normally carried backwards close against the body, but it is capable of movement in any direction or angle. The female retains a normal anal fin.

You will recognise courtship by the alert appearance of the male, who, with fins erect,

Hyphessobrycon rosaceus

chases the female until a suitable opportunity presents itself for a quick thrust of the gonopodium.

Livebearers rarely seem to need any artificial means of inducing them to breed. On the contrary, they usually breed quicker than accommodation can be found.

Females can have up to eight broods from one fertilisation, therefore it is not necessary to mate them immediately after the first brood. One school of thought suggests that if a male is put with a female within 24 hours of delivery of her young, the next brood will be influenced by the last male, but I do not completely accept this view. It is unlikely it will have any effect on the subsequent broods until after the fifth. Better control of fertilisation can be maintained if the sexes are kept in separate tanks to prevent cross breeding among similar species.

A 'ripe' female is one that is almost ready to give birth. You can determine this by the dark crescent-shaped area on the female's body close to the vent, known as the 'gravid spot'. This is accompanied by a fattening of the fish when viewed from the top or side. After a little practice it is possible to judge from these two factors roughly the time of delivery.

The number of young in a brood is influenced by size; the larger the female the greater number of fry per brood. This has no effect, however, on the size of the babies, which are all born approximately the same size.

Livebearers are cannibalistic, and have no hesitation in devouring their own young as soon as they are born. You can prevent this by putting the ripe female into a tank by herself with plenty of fine leaf foliage (*Myriophyllum*) in which the young can take refuge. Remove the female as soon as the young are born.

It is not always possible for the business man to be on hand to remove the female when it would do most good, and to overcome this difficulty I advise you to use a maternity cage or breeding trap. The object of the trap is to restrict the female to a portion of the aquarium by means of a Perspex cage, the bottom of which is made up of a series of rods spaced so that newly born fry will fall through out of reach. When suspended from the aquarium side, the top edge should be $\frac{1}{2}$ in. above water level.

A great advantage of the breeding cage is that more than one female can be put into it simultaneously without fear of one eating the fry of the other, as they are delivered.

Another method of safeguarding the young is to insert two pieces of glass or Perspex in the

Gasteropelecus levis
Barbus everetti

tank to form a trough, with a gap of $\frac{1}{8}$ in. along the bottom edges for the fry to fall through. A bracket made from sheet lead, notched to hold the glass will keep it in position, or make a trough completely of glass using Araldite as an adhesive.

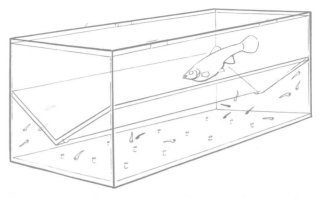

The advantage of such a trap is its easy installation when required.

Generally snails should always be present in the tanks, if feeding dry food, to eat up any surplus. Snails need access to air, so do not fill the tank to such an extent that there is no surface area between the trap and the side of the aquarium. (See also filters.)

Handling of livebearers when they are near the time of delivery may cause them to give birth prematurely. Premature young have not fully absorbed the yolk sac, which can be seen attached to the belly. Few premature births survive, but if the yolk sac is very small they may be saved by adding one teaspoonful of salt to every gallon of water.

For feeding of fry see page 44.

Egg-laying tooth carps and egg-layers

The egg-laying tooth carps are easily distinguished from the live-bearing tooth carps by the absence of the external sex organ, the gonopodium. They are not quite so easily bred, but the satisfaction of a good spawning gives a greater sense of achievement.

The following description of spawning by the egg-layers can be taken as a generality, for, in most cases, the spawnings are similar, but where specific departures from this occur, they will be dealt with under the heading of the species.

For the egg-laying tooth carps, your aquarium should be prepared with dense thickets of fine-leaved plants with plenty of open space to allow them to chase.

Willow root is an excellent medium for protecting eggs in the spawning tank, it forms a dense mat into which the eggs can fall. Make

55

certain that the root is boiled before introducing it into the breeding tank. The advantage of willow root is that it can be stored and used whenever required.

Sexes that have been kept separate are more likely to spawn readily, but if accommodation is so limited that it prevents this, separate them three or four days before introducing them to the breeding tank.

Healthy strong fish produce the best offspring, so feed them rather more frequently than usual for about a week before mating with scrapings of raw meat, daphnia, shrimp, earthworm, and small quantities of dried prepared food.

Introduce the female a day in advance of the male to let her acclimatise herself to the new surroundings. When the male is put in he may seem rather shy at first, but it will not be long before courtship takes place. This takes the form of repeated dashes about the tank accompanied by various actions like fin nibbling, and quivering side by side.

Eggs dropped amongst the plants by the female are fertilised by milt ejected from the male. At the completion of the spawning, both parents or the plants to which the eggs are attached should be removed to another tank, bearing in mind the temperatures should be consistent. This prevents the parents eating the eggs.

The incubation varies with different species. When the eggs hatch the young look like an egg to which a fine body is attached to the top, and as the fish develop, the egg-like appendage, which is the yolk-sac, becomes absorbed. The yolk-sac provides nourishment in the first stages before the fish are able to swim and spend their time keeping out of harm's way hopping about on the sandy bottom, or clinging to the glass sides of the aquarium.

It is this stage, the early feeding period, that is the most critical. The table on page 44 shows how to feed fry. It is as well to start a culture of infusoria as soon as the spawning takes place, so that it is available when needed. It is difficult to state how much infusoria should be given as it varies so much in quality. Experience will provide the best guide. However, the feeding should be frequent, so that the bellies of the fry visibly bulge.

You will notice that some of the youngsters will develop more quickly than others. Probably some are born more energetic, and get the original advantage by eating the most and best food.

Anabantids (bubble nesters)

Anabantids are the family of labyrinthic fish. They possess special accessory organs for breathing atmospheric air, and are consequently not so easily affected by overcrowding.

The name labyrinth is derived from the intricate network of capillaries in the auxiliary breathing apparatus, which is comparable to a lung in animals. These capillaries are brought into contact with air actually taken from the atmosphere.

Breathing is not the slow rhythmical process of the normal lung: oxygen is absorbed from a bubble of air taken into the mouth, retained for a while, and then expelled through the gills. A fresh bubble is taken in simultaneously with the expulsion of the old one.

Bubble nesters do not breathe continually in this manner. Conditions of environment, oxygen content of water, and so on, all affect the use of the secondary organ. They are not a particularly large family, and most of them are quite suitable for aquarium use. As a matter of interest *Osphronemus gourami*, one of the largest gouramis, attain a weight of over 20 lb.

As most of the Anabantids are bubble nesters, and breed much to the same pattern, the following description on breeding can be taken generally, any peculiarity to a species will be covered under the species heading to save repitition.

The nest is built by the male, either in a corner of the aquarium, under floating plants, or even under a single leaf. The fish rises to the surface, takes in a mouthful of air, and envelopes it in a sticky saliva-like fluid, which, when expelled, floats to the surface. By continuing this action the bubble nester forms a dome shaped mound of sticky whitish bubbles.

At breeding time the species usually becomes pugnacious which may result in the death of one of them, and it usually turns out to be the female. For this reason your breeding tank should be thickly planted to offer a refuge to the female. Breeding pairs should be roughly the same size, and well fed on live foods. They take quite well to dry foods, but prefer something moving.

When the male starts to build the nest, you know he is ready to breed. If the pairs are not already together, it is time to introduce them by putting the male into the tank already occupied by his mate. You can recognise courtship by the heightened colour and activity of the male, who uses every wile to attract the female beneath the nest. Eventually she succumbs to his charm. Should she be slow to respond he becomes impatient, tearing her fins and attacking her in a most pugnacious manner. This, of course, is when she is most likely to meet her death. There is naturally a certain amount of boisterousness during this period, but should it become likely to result in death, removal of the male is advised. Give them another trial at a later date.

In a normal courtship, when the female is under the nest, the male wraps himself around the female in a nuptial embrace until the spawn is released.

This is immediately fertilised, and drops to the bottom of the tank. Now the male picks the eggs up and blows them into the sticky mass of bubble where they remain.

The spawning consists of repeated embraces and insertions of eggs into the nest, which will eventually number between 100 and 500. At this stage, the female should be removed, for the eggs are now cared for by father, who will resent any interference from her, charging her away from the vicinity of the nest.

During the next two or three days the nest will have the undivided attention of the male, who will renew burst bubbles and replace eggs that fall. The nest will become noticeably larger.

In approximately two days, the eggs will hatch. The young will then be no more than small black dots. Some will fall from the nest, only to be quickly returned by the ever-vigilant father. After about three days, the yolk-sac will be absorbed and you will see the fry swimming about just below the surface. At this stage you should feed infusoria. The fry will now become more active, and spread more widely around the tank clinging to the glass, and the task of keeping them together will be more difficult for their hard-worked parent.

As the fry develop so the male will lose interest. He is then quite likely to forget all the trouble he has taken to protect them, and eat them, and it is at this time he should be removed. You can now rear the fry on infusoria followed by micro-worm, etc.

You will find that a cover over the aquarium prevents evaporation of the nest and protects the fry from draughts when they are at a critical stage of their development, but care should be taken that the cover is suitably tilted to allow condensation to run back into the tank away from the nest, otherwise drops of water falling on the nest will break it up.

Cichlids

Cichlids have spiny-rayed fins. In general they are larger and more quarrelsome than the other fish in this book, and consequently they can hardly be regarded as good citizens for a community aquarium, although a number of large specimens in a tank seem to be compatible enough. The following breeding description will fit most species, but where there is any difference it will be noted under the species heading.

The Cichlids are good parents, looking after their young with infinite care and the whole breeding cycle is most interesting to observe. Selection of mates is of considerable importance for,

like humans, fish have a natural affinity towards each other. If you put a pair into the breeding tank and they become 'bad friends', it will probably result in the death of one of them.

A tank no smaller than 24 in. × 12 in. × 12 in. is the most suitable size. You should spread clean sand on the bottom to a depth of 2 in., and use well-seasoned water, but do not plant, for the plants will soon be uprooted. Two slots cut in the centre of the top aquarium frame allow a glass partition to be inserted making two separate compartments. Put the male in one side, and the female in the other. If they are obviously prepared to mate, the partition can be removed. Readiness for courtship may be recognised by a wagging of the body, spreading of fins, and general changing of colour. Either fish may make the first advance, and when the other responds in like manner it is safe to remove the partition. If a number of the same species are kept in one tank, some will naturally pair. These should then be removed to the breeding tank, and it will then not be necessary to put in a partition.

If the courtship goes to plan, the next stage will consist of 'kissing'. They hold each other by the lips and start a lively tug of war. They may repeat this action several times. Should both of the Cichlids stand the trial and neither weaken, it is safe to assume they will mate, but should one panic or lose its nerve, it is liable to be killed by its mate. Removal of one is then advised, but a later try may prove successful. It will be seen that it is an advantage to mate fish as near as possible of like size.

All being well the fish will be observed during the next two or three days digging holes in the sand and cleaning a suitable place to lay their eggs. They seem to have a preference for light-coloured surfaces, so a flat lightish-coloured stone should be placed on the bottom. Some aquarists use marble, or a flower pot laid on its side.

Cleanliness is the byword, the spot selected to receive the adhesive eggs is thoroughly cleaned with the mouth. A few days before the actual spawning, both sexes develop an ovipositor, or breeding tube, which first appears as a small protrusion on the underside of the belly and increases in length shortly before actual breeding.

The female hovers over the stone, or spot selected, touching it with the breeding tube, and at the same time deposits one or two eggs. The male immediately follows and with a similar action fertilises the eggs by spraying them with milt. This action is repeated until 100 to 1,000 eggs are deposited. The fish now take turns fanning the eggs with the breast fins and tail, relieving each other every few minutes. The accepted idea of fanning is that it keeps the eggs clean and supplies oxygen to the embryos. Eggs hatch in four days at a temperature of 80° F.

Just before or soon after the eggs hatch, they are transferred in the mouths of the parents to a hollow in the sand. The young are not easy to see, and look like a moving jelly-like mass.

During the next few days, the infant Cichlids will find themselves gently transferred from one depression to another. It takes between four to ten days for the yolk-sacs to become absorbed, after which you can see the young swimming freely in a school. Recalcitrant youngsters are quickly gathered up in the mouths of the parents and put back in the school.

The fry, after absorbing the yolk-sac, are large enough to eat brine shrimps, micro-worms, or sifted daphnia.

Whilst it is a pretty sight to see the parents and babies swimming around the tank together, their parents should not be allowed to remain too long lest they misinterpret some action of their owner as a danger signal, and eat the fry.

Live-bearing tooth carps

The live-bearing tooth carps, belong to the super-order Atherinomorpha, sub-order Cyprinodontoidei and are grouped under the family Poeciliidae (live-bearing tooth carps). They are all readily identifiable by the elongated gonopodium of the male, which replaces the more normal anal fin. It is mainly the differences in this organ that decides the various generic classifications.

All Poeciliidae are found in the New World.

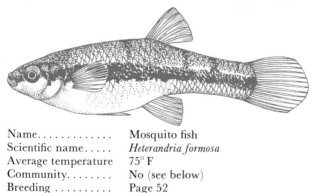

Name	Mosquito fish
Scientific name	*Heterandria formosa*
Average temperature	75° F
Community	No (see below)
Breeding	Page 52
Reproduction	Viviparous
Natural location	N. Carolina to Florida

This is one of the smallest fish known to science, the males being only ¾-in. long. The females are slightly larger, about 1⅛ in. Their principal colouring is olive-brown with black markings. Owing to the tiny size of the mosquito fish, they are best kept in an aquarium of their own, or at least in a tank containing only fish of a similar size.

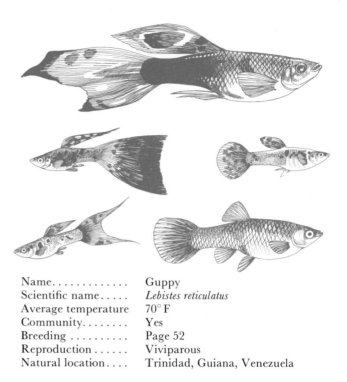

Name	Guppy
Scientific name	*Lebistes reticulatus*
Average temperature	70° F
Community	Yes
Breeding	Page 52
Reproduction	Viviparous
Natural location	Trinidad, Guiana, Venezuela

This marvellous little fish is a beauty, so much so that many aquarists specialise and breed nothing else but guppies. It is usually the first species obtained, and no matter how far advanced the aquarist becomes, a few guppies will always be found in his collection.

To describe the coloration would be almost an impossibility, for rarely, if ever, are two marked the same—in fact, for this reason, they are also known as rainbow fish.

The male only is the possessor of this beautiful colouring, which may be any combination of blue, green, yellow, and red, with characteristic dark markings superimposed, including a dark spot about midway along the side of the body, or on the dorsal fin, sometimes both.

The dorsal fin varies greatly in length, sometimes it is comparatively short in length, at other times it streams out over the tail.

The average length of the male is 1⅛ in., but the female is much larger, up to 2¼ in., and in no way does she resemble the male in coloration. Her body colour is a fishy silver, which can be tinged with another colour depending upon breeding. For instance, the golden guppy female has a suffusion of pale orange covering the body.

The main attraction of the guppy is its adaptability. Extremely hardy, it can stand wide ranges of temperatures. It has several other virtues—it is easy to feed, it can stand overcrowding, it is not pugnacious or timid, it is a prolific breeder, and the young mature rapidly. The last is a great asset to those interested in breeding particular strains.

The caudal fin varies considerably in shape from

a full round to a top or bottom sword. These swords are, in fact, actual extensions of the fins, and stream out behind the fish.

By carefully selected line breeding, many of the characteristic markings have become farily well fixed. These include the top and bottom 'sword-tail', 'lyre tail', 'spear tail', 'pin tail', 'round tail', 'cofertail', 'lace', 'peacock', 'robson', 'scarftail', etc.

In Britain, the Guppy Breeders' Society is devoted solely to this colourful fish. It publishes its own magazine, and it has been established that over 200,000 people in the United Kingdom keep guppies.

Although the guppy can stand wide temperature ranges, no attempt should be made to keep them under any conditions other than tropical. Their breeding period is considerably lengthened with lower temperatures, and accelerated by high temperatures (by high, 80° F is intended). Frequent feeding of smallish amounts is better than one large feed a day, and plenty of live foods should be included in the diet.

They breed in the manner described on page 52 and the number of young can vary from six to sixty depending upon size and condition.

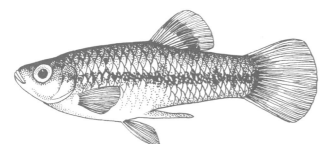

Name	Blue poecilia
Scientific name	*Limia caudofasciata*
Average temperature	75° F
Community	Yes
Breeding	Page 52
Reproduction	Viviparous
Natural location	Jamaica

The general body colour is olive, with dark markings along the sides, these provide an ideal background for the metallic blue spots flecking the surface of the body. The dorsal fin of the male is yellow-orange and has a dark spot at the base. Fins of the female are clear except for a slight yellow coloration at the base of the dorsal. The belly of the male is slightly golden. Both sexes have golden eyes.

This species is truly a beautiful aquarium fish. It is vividly coloured, and is shown to its best advantage by reflected light and with a number of them together in a single tank.

Males grow to about 1½-in. long and females grow to 2¼-in. long. They are peaceful and hardy,

but when breeding they have a tendency to eat the fry, so use a breeding trap or plenty of suitable plants.

Name	
Scientific name	*Limia melanogaster*
Average temperature	75° F
Community	Yes
Breeding	Page 52
Reproduction	Viviparous
Natural location	Jamaica

Although very similar in many respects to *L. caudofasciata*, this species has a body colour tending towards brown, or brownish olive green. It is marked with dark vertical bars on the rear half of the body. The number of bars may vary from five to eight, but generally there are about six.

The dorsal fin of the male is pale yellow marked with two dark bands—one on the margin, the other on the base. This fin on the female is clear, and only carries the dark base marking. The caudal fin of the male is deep orange with a dark band.

Adult females attain a length of about 2½ in. and males about 2 in.

Name	Hump-back limia
Scientific name	*Limia nigrofasciata*
Average temperature	75° F
Community	Yes
Breeding	Page 52
Reproduction	Viviparous
Natural location	Haiti

Unfortunately, as the male matures its body outline becomes less attractive. The black-edged dorsal fin enlarges, and the forepart of the back developes a decided hump.

Body colour is blue-green, the upper part of the body being marked indistinctly with dark vertical bars. There may also be dark marks on the caudal fin. Females are somewhat lighter in colour, and attain a length of 2½ in., males only to about 2 in. This species will eat soft green algæ, which should be available as part of their normal diet.

These fish are active and peaceful. They breed readily at a temperature of about 73° F.

59

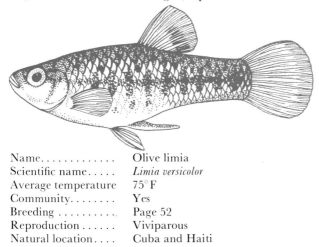

Name	Green poecilid
Scientific name	*Limia ornata*
Average temperature	75°F
Community	Yes
Breeding	Page 52
Reproduction	Viviparous
Natural location	Haiti

This species is very similar to *L. caudofasciata*. It is hardy, peaceful, and very colourful. The body is yellow-green, mottled with irregular black spots, and it has silver-edged scales. The dorsal fin of the male is usually red and spotted with black. The anal and caudal fins are also black spotted.

Males attain a length between 1½ and 2 in.; females are somewhat larger, up to 3 in.

Name	Olive limia
Scientific name	*Limia versicolor*
Average temperature	75°F
Community	Yes
Breeding	Page 52
Reproduction	Viviparous
Natural location	Cuba and Haiti

The body colour of *L. versicolor* is a reddish olive-brown, slightly darker on the back, graduating to a silvery white on the belly. It is marked with a blue stripe along the body and with vertical dark bars, mainly on the rear half of the body. Both dorsal and caudal fins are yellow, and occasionally the caudal fin will be found marked with vertical bands. There is invariably a dark spot on the base of the dorsal fin.

Females usually grow to a length of about 2½ in., and males to about 1¾ in.

Name	Striped mud fish
Scientific name	*Limia vittata*
Average temperature	75°F
Community	Yes
Breeding	Page 52
Reproduction	Viviparous
Natural location	Cuba

These fish are not particularly attractive, and their relatively large size is considered to be a disadvantage by some aquarists. Males grow to about 2½ in., and females to about 3¾ in. The colour of the body is olive-brown which reflects a blue sheen. The sides of the male are generally marked with irregular, dark vertical bars, broken in places, on the rear of the body, but these markings may well be absent entirely. Both sexes may have horizontal lines formed by dark dots. Both the dorsal and tail fins are tinted yellow. Only the male has dark markings on these fins.

It is a hardy, peaceful livebearer that breeds readily.

Name	Sail-fin mollie
Scientific name	*Mollienisia latipinna*
Average temperature	70°F
Community	Yes
Breeding	Page 52
Reproduction	Viviparous
Natural location	N. Carolina, Florida, N.E. Mexico

The sail-fin mollie, gets its name from the large dorsal fin that extends the length of the back of the male, and which on a good specimen is as high as the fish is deep. Unfortunately, the quality and size varies greatly, and unless you obtain a really excellent specimen it will not be an outstanding exhibit.

As with all large-finned fish, it is most impressive when the fins are erect. The dorsal then shows an iridescent blue, and the caudal becomes lightish blue with a yellow streak through the centre.

During courtship the display of colour is at its best. Body tints are of an olive colour, with narrow brown stripes running laterally along the sides, which are separated by lines of a lighter hue and of a somewhat jagged pattern.

Largely vegetarian, the mollies should be kept in a tank with plenty of light to encourage growth of soft green algæ, which they continually eat. If the growth is insufficient, it can be taken from another tank. A good substitute for algæ is boiled spinach. Feed little and often is the requirement. Dried shrimp, Bemax, and occasionally daphnia and tubifex will keep all of them healthy.

Generally more care must be taken as unskilful netting of ripe females often causes the young to be stillborn or defective. Do not use a breeding trap. Mollies need plenty of room, and a breeding trap does not allow that. Fine-leafed plants in thick profusion will afford the young sufficient refuge. Breeding temperature is 78° F, and they prefer slightly alkaline water.

Permablack Mollienisia

Originally, the amazing all black mollie was line bred from natural freaks and is actually a variety of *M. latipinna*, or *M. sphenops*.

The colouring, a deep velvety black, covers the whole body; even the eyes are hard to distinguish. Some specimens have an orange fringe to the caudal fin, but the most sought after ones are completely black.

The young are born larger than those of the average livebearer, and are completely black at birth, but most of them become lighter after a few weeks, and when about an inch in length the black begins to return in spots. After a period of about 6 months, some go entirely black, whilst others remain motted all their lives.

Name	Giant sail-fin mollie
Scientific name	*Mollienisia velifera*
Average temperature	75° F
Community	Yes
Breeding	Page 52
Reproduction	Viviparous
Natural location	Yucatan

As may be expected from the popular name of this fish, the large dorsal fin is its most prominent characteristic. It has a general body colour of brilliant blue-green, peppered with sparkling spots. The belly and throat are golden to yellow. The magnificent dorsal of the male is green-blue with a purple sheen and it is marked most attractively with blue, red, brown and orange patterning. The female is not so brilliantly coloured and has a smaller dorsal fin.

Good aquarium specimens can attain a length of about 4 in.

The young are about $\frac{1}{2}$ in. at birth and can number up to 100 in a single brood. They develop fairly rapidly, but the full beauty of the dorsal may take up to 12 months to develop.

When breeding remember that the parents are likely to devour the fry, so provide adequate protection with plants, or a breeding trap.

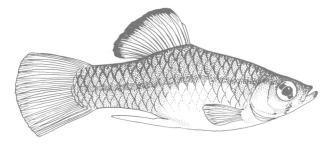

Name	Merry widow
Scientific name	*Phallichthys amates*
Average temperature	70° F
Community	Yes
Breeding	Page 52
Reproduction	Viviparous
Natural location	Honduras

Because of the thin black line edging the dorsal fin, which is similar to that of a mourning card, this delightful little fish has been given the popular name of merry widow.

Females, like the guppies, are twice as large as the males, but lack the subtle beauty of the dorsal fin. This fin, which is usually carried proudly erect, is marked with two arcs parallel to the outside edge. Both arcs are dark but the inner one is slightly lighter.

Other markings are narrow, dark vertical lines along the body, which is a shade of olive green, and a short black line that passes through the eye. Their gill covers reflect an iridescent blue-green, and this colour can also be detected on the body when caught by the light.

Another outstanding feature of the merry widow is the long gonopodium. The latin generic name of *Phallichthys* means fish with phallus or gonopodium.

Always a lively fish, the merry widow can be relied upon for constant animation of the aquarium.

Breeding is quite easily accomplished at a temperature of 78° F.

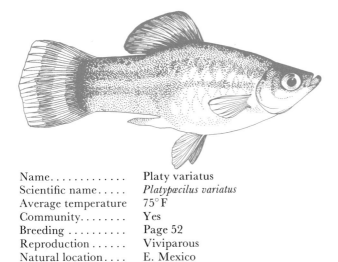

Name. . . . . Platy variatus
Scientific name. . . . . *Platypœcilus variatus*
Average temperature 75°F
Community. . . . . Yes
Breeding . . . . Page 52
Reproduction . . . . . . Viviparous
Natural location. . . . E. Mexico

This species was first collected and used for aquaria in the early 1930s, and has been a firm favourite ever since. It should not be confused with the *P. maculatus*.

The male is not smaller than the female. Both, when fully grown, attain a length of approximately 2 in. It is in the colouring that the main difference occurs. Females usually have a dull brownish green body with a dark zigzag line along the sides, and only the male boasts the gorgeous variegated colours which can combine yellow, blue, red, and green on one fish.

Breeding is easy, but it is not so easy to obtain a large proportion of excellently coloured males per brood. In an average hatching of, say, 30, only ten will be males, of which perhaps only three will be well coloured, and in any case it will be eight to ten months before any real colour begins to show.

When selecting pairs for breeding, you should never choose a small male—the bigger and brighter coloured, the better. Females should be selected by their body colour—the deeper the better.

Young are born four to five weeks after fertilisation, and with a fully grown female should number between sixty and eighty. Instead of the breeding trap, fine-leafed plants with some floating duckweed or riccia will ensure better results. Shallow water about 6-in. deep is advisable so that fry can reach the surface easily.

Given plenty of room and ample good food, the young should grow to 1 in. in about twelve weeks.

It is interesting to note that up to eight broods can be the result of one fertilisation. These broods are born approximately once a month, but the water temperature has a bearing on the period. If the temperature is below 75°F, the intervening

Mollienisia latipinna

Permablack mollienisia

period will be longer.

Platys prefer slightly acid water, about pH 6·8.

Name. . . . . Platy (various)
Scientific name. . . . . *Platypœcilus maculatus*
Average temperature 75°F
Community. . . . . Yes
Breeding . . . . Page 52
Reproduction . . . . . . Viviparous
Natural location. . . . Rio Papaloapan, S. Mexico

Here is a species that combines all that is desirable in a good aquarium fish—it is peaceful, easily bred, and can be obtained in such a wide variety of colour that it is almost unbelievable. In addition to these qualifications, the platy has provided a most interesting variety of hybrids.

This species is also known as 'moonfish' because of the dark crescent-shaped marking on the base of the tail of early importations.

The males grow to about 1½ in. and females 2 in.

Use natural vegetation during breeding instead of the breeding trap, as the platys much prefer it. They can, however, be bred in the trap, but the use of a trap does not give the best results. Platys breed indiscriminately—they have no preference for colour, a red variety is quite likely to mate with a wagtail, with the result that the fry are nondescript.

Care should be taken to keep pure strains separate, or at least the sexes in different tanks so that undesirable crosses cannot take place. Any crosses or hybridising should be under the strict control of their owner. When mating choose only the best specimens.

They are rather fond of algæ, so you should let them have a supply of it.

Probably the most outstanding variety of platy is the wagtail. This is one of the latest types to reach the aquarist. It was developed by Dr. Myron Gordon by crossing a wild comet platy with the domesticated golden platy. At first all the fins were black and the body was coloured a dull golden-grey in the original breeding, but now in addition to the black fins a better body colouring, red and gold, is quite common.

The young do not develop the complete black fin coloration until approximately six weeks after they are born, but it is discernible in streaks as soon as they are born.

The red platy is a truly beautiful colour of dark orange with a tinge of brown adding a richness. In young fish the colour is not so deep, but it improves, like good wine, with age.

Unfortunately, this species is not too hardy, and whilst they thrive in one aquarium they may degenerate if they are moved into another. There seems to be no explanation for this.

The golden platy is actually a deep yellow in

colour with a translucent quality that makes the fish seem frail. They have red dorsals and a black crescent at the tail root.

The blue variety covers a wide range of shades, even green.

Remember when breeding that they do not respect the colour of a possible mate and will 'colour mix' readily.

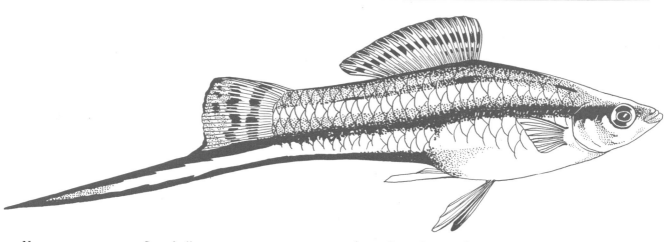

Name............	Swordtail
Scientific name.....	*Xiphophorus hellerii*
Average temperature	70°F
Community........	Yes
Breeding..........	Page 52
Reproduction......	Viviparous
Natural location....	E. Mexico

The swordtail is a good showy aquarium fish which is always lively and provides a continuous source of interest for its owners.

Originally the colouring was of a greenish hue, with a metallic green tail spike and a distinct red line along the centre of the body, but by careful breeding and hybridising many colour variations are now available.

The red variety, obtained by hybridising with a red platy, has a deep orange body and long tail spike varying from orange to yellow, bordered with a thin black line.

Coloration in the green variety is particularly pleasing, the green hue getting lighter as it approaches the underside of the body and the red lateral marking being further enhanced by the addition of a yellowish band above it.

Albino swords are usually of a lightish colour and the sword-like tail fin is also of a lighter hue than with other varieties, and like all true albinos the eyes are pink.

Sexing is easy for in addition to the gonopodium only the males have a long extension to their tails.

This species has a tendency to bully, so for the sake of peace it is best to have only one sizeable male in the aquarium. They are good jumpers, so do not leave the aquarium uncovered otherwise they are likely to be found on the floor next morning.

They are fond of algæ, and it is advisable to have some available even if it means scraping it off the glass of another tank.

They breed in the manner described on page 52, except that care should be taken not to chill the fish as this often has a lasting effect with this species. Breeding temperature is 80°F. The number of young per female is in the region of 100 to 150, providing the female is large.

Swordtails prefer slightly alkaline water.

Livebearer hybrids

A hybrid is the result of two different species mating.

In the fish world this mainly occurs among the live-bearing species. The reason for this seems to be that they lack the reserve of their fellow egg-layers. Observation of the guppy, for instance, will soon convince the onlooker that it is strongly endowed with the sex instinct. If a male is unlucky enough to find himself in a tank without females of his own species, it is quite likely that he will endeavour to mate with another, even an egg-layer. It is not possible for *any* species of fish to cross indiscriminately, as they have to be closely related for fertilisation to take effect. The more distant the relationship, the more unlikely the fertilisation. However, if a cross should occur between distantly related fish, the resulting fry are almost certainly to be defective and will, in all probability, die quickly. This is Nature's way of ensuring that only the best survive to carry on the species.

The best known hybrids are probably crosses between *Platypœcilus maculatus* and *Xiphophorus hellerii* (platy and swordtail), which result in such

Platypoecilus maculatus

64

interesting fish as the black spangled—a beautiful fish, generally black but reflecting a blue-green sheen; and the calico—a fish probably produced by crossing a black spangled with a hybrid red swordtail.

Aquarists wishing to indulge in this type of breeding should be careful to ensure that only virgin females are used. As previously mentioned, one fertilisation can result in more than one brood of fry, so unless virgin females are used the results must be uncertain.

Fish intended for hybridisation should be segregated very early, even before they show sex indications, and kept in separate jars. When the sexes are known, the females can then be put into an aquarium to be selected for breeding as required.

Egg-laying tooth carps

The egg-laying tooth carps belong to the super-order Atherinomorpha, sub-order Cyprinodontoidei and are grouped under the family Cyprinodontoidae (egg-laying tooth carps, top-minnows or killifish). The majority of fish described in this section belong to the sub-family Funduline, which has one pointed tooth. The few exceptions are *Jordanella* and *Aphanius*, which are grouped under the sub-family Cyprinodontinae and which has three pointed teeth.

There are, in fact, over 200 recorded species of Cyprinodontinae.

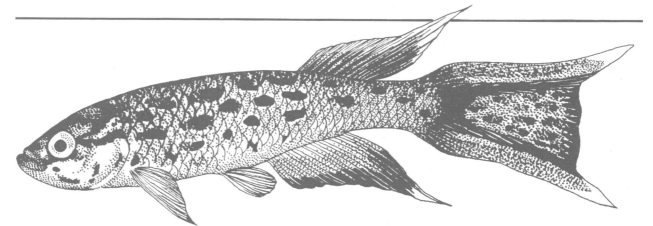

Name	Lyretail
Scientific name	*Aphyosemion australe*
Average temperature	74°F
Community	Yes
Breeding	See below
Reproduction	Oviparous
Natural location	West Africa

The male lyretail is a particularly handsome fellow. The general body colour is a light brownish-green, darkening on the back to sepia, and lightening to bluish-green on the belly. The body is spotted with irregular carmine marks. Both the dorsal and anal fins are edged with a carmine and blue-green stripe. As may be expected, the tail is most beautiful, the outer rays are pink to orange terminating in white tips and within the outer rays two broad stripes of carmine form a box-like pattern encompassing a blue-green panel and this is spotted with carmine dots. The outer rays of the tail, dorsal and anal fins reduce into filaments.

The female has a similar body colour, and is marked with a few carmine spots on the body and unpaired fins, otherwise she is relatively plain.

This species grow to about 2½ in. in length. They must be kept in slightly acid old water of pH 6·8. The breeding temperature should be 78°F, and the eggs hatch in 12–14 days. The eggs are unlikely to be eaten by the adults, but remove them when the spawning has been completed as a precautionary measure.

Name	Banded fundulus
Scientific name	*Aphyosemion bivittatum*
Average temperature	73°F
Community	Yes
Breeding	See below
Reproduction	Oviparous
Natural location	Tropical West Africa

The body colour is yellow-brown marked with crimson spots. There is a dark stripe extending from the nose, through the eye, and along the body to the tail root. A second stripe extends from below the eye, along the lower part of the body and terminates also on the tail root. The dorsal fin is beautifully marked with crimson spots near the base, and streaked with the same colour on the tip. The anal and caudal fins are marked similarly.

The fins are more developed and better marked on the male. This is particularly true of the caudal fin which has extending filaments on the upper and lower lobes.

This species must be kept in old water, pH 7·5. The fish will not take kindly to even slightly new water, and they do require a carnivorous diet,

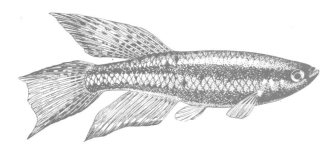

preferably live.

They are a little difficult to keep successfully and not too easy to breed. However, neither is impossible.

Eggs are deposited among clumps of plants and hatch in about 12 days. The ideal breeding temperature is about 72°F and the water should be slightly saline.

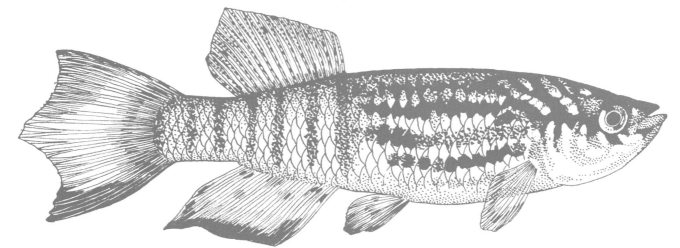

Name............	Blue gularis
Scientific name.....	*Aphyosemion coeruleum*
Average temperature	73°F
Community........	Yes (only if with fish of like size)
Breeding..........	Page 55
Reproduction......	Oviparous
Natural location....	West Africa

Blue gularis vary somewhat in colour, but generally the body is a yellow-brown that darkens on the back, and lightens to a blue white on the belly. The lips and gill covers are blue but the gill covers are also marked with red streaks. These streaks are also present on the fore part of the body. The rear of the body is marked with red dots, together with a few vertical bars. The dorsal fin is green-blue and tinged with red at the base, the somewhat large anal fin is greenish, dotted red, and blue fringed. The caudal fin is reasonably large and has three 'tails'. The upper is blue marked with red dots and streaks; the middle is red and yellow; and the lower is blue-green streaked with red. Females are paler in colour.

An overall colour effect of blue is experienced when viewing this species in a good light. This is not strictly a community fish; it prefers rather special conditions, and although it is not a troublesome species, it has a decided liking for fish small enough to be eaten.

It much prefers old water at a temperature not in excess of 74°F. It does not like to be subjected to very strong light.

Aquariums containing blue gularis should be covered to prevent the fish jumping out. Adult fish grow to about 4½ in.

Remember this species is carnivorous and should only be fed with live foods.

Breeding temperature should be about 70°F. Eggs are laid singly either on, or near, the bottom, and can take a long time to hatch. Fry are not difficult to raise.

Name............	Yellow gularis
Scientific name.....	*Aphyosemion gulare*
Average temperature	73°F
Community........	Yes
Breeding..........	See below
Reproduction......	Oviparous
Natural location....	West Africa

This species is very similar in many respects to the blue gularis, in fact the blue gularis is believed to be a larger sub-species of a *A. gulare*. The latter is only about 2½-in. long when adult.

Body colour is yellow to pale brown marked by dark reddish brown mottling on the fore part of the body, which modifies gradually into vertical bars at the rear of the body. The dorsal fin has a red line and carmine flecks. The anal fin is pale yellow, flecked with carmine. The caudal fin is red, streaked with red-brown on the lower part.

Females are generally less colourful with less mottlings and have colourless fins.

It breeds in a similar manner to *A. coeruleum*, but not so readily.

Live foods should be the staple diet of this species, as it is strictly carnivorous. However, it might occasionally take a mouthful of dried food.

67

Name............	Argentine pearl fish
Scientific name.....	*Cynolebias bellottii*
Average temperature	70°F
Community........	Yes
Breeding..........	See below
Reproduction......	Oviparous
Natural location....	La Plata

Name............	— —
Scientific name.....	*Epiplatys chaperi*
Average temperature	70°F
Community........	Yes
Breeding..........	See below
Reproduction......	Oviparous
Natural location....	West Africa

This attractive species is also known as the blue chromide. The male has a general body colour of dark slatey-blue which changes to blue-green on the fins. The body and fins are speckled with pearly-white spots.

Females are ochre or yellow-green, marked irregularly with brownish stripes similar to the graining on marble. The margins of the males' anal, caudal and dorsal fins are dark. Both sexes have a dark stripe through the eye.

Under natural conditions these fish breed in ditches and puddles during the rainy season. The male makes a small depression in the mud, and into the depression the female deposits a single egg which is immediately fertilised and covered by the male. This performance is then repeated. When the pools dry out, the parents perish, but the eggs are protected by the damp mud and remain dormant until the next rains come. The eggs then hatch out and the cycle is continued.

Breeding in an aquarium requires a temperature of 72°F and slightly brackish water (one teaspoonful of sea-salt per gallon should be added to the aquarium).

After spawning, remove the adults and drain the aquarium gradually over a period of ten days. Leave the sand moist and the tank empty for about three weeks. Then refill over a period of three to four days with clean rain water. The young should hatch in about two days. Feed with brine shrimps or sifted daphnia.

Rearing the fry is not particularly difficult; provided they are well fed with live food they will reach adult size within eight weeks.

It is rather surprising that this species is not more popular in this country, for it is easily fed, extremely pretty, and offers quite interesting breeding habits.

The male is the most handsome, with diffused vertical bars along the side of body, and dark edging to the anal fin and base of the caudal fin. The throat and lower lip, best seen from the front, are a fiery red. A peculiarity that makes the sexes easily distinguishable is the pointed extension to the caudal fin of the male.

For breeding *E. chaperi*, a loose-floating plant like *Riccia* is needed in addition to normal plants. The aquarium should be placed in a position where it will not get too much sunlight. The best results are obtained if two females are used to one male. The temperature should be raised to 77°F and the females introduced a couple of days in advance of the male.

The female will probably be a little shy at first, but this soon disappears when the male drives her into the masses of *Riccia*, where they remain side by side and a single egg is dropped and fertilised. The females drop only one egg at a time, 15 to 20 being an average for a day. After about a week the spawning ends.

The eggs are about the size of a pin head, and although they are not usually eaten by the parents at this stage, it is advisable to remove the plants with eggs attached, or the parents before the young hatch. Put them into a large jar and stand in the aquarium to maintain the temperature.

It is important for the eggs to be kept in subdued light, as strong light is harmful. The eggs hatch in about two weeks. Remember that there will be a difference in ages of one week, so the young will be correspondingly different in sizes. They should be transferred to a tank with only 5 in. of water in depth, until strong enough for a greater depth, usually about a month.

Mild aeration helps at this stage. Infusoria need only be fed for a short time; graduation on to brine shrimps ensures rapid growth.

Rivulus cylindraceus and *Panchax lineatus* are also species which breed in this manner.

E. chaperi prefer slightly alkaline water about pH 7·1.

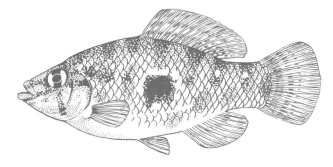

Name	Flag fish
Scientific name	*Jordanella floridæ*
Average temperature	70° F
Community	Yes (if not put with smaller fish)
Breeding	Page 55
Reproduction	Oviparous
Natural location	Florida

The name flag fish was bestowed upon this species because of its resemblance to the American flag. The scale edging is red in colour, corresponding in some degree to the stars on the American flag. In appearance and habit it is rather like a sunfish.

The flag fish will eat live foods, but it is more of a vegetarian, and to keep it in condition conducive to breeding, algæ should always be available. If this is difficult to obtain, boiled spinach is a good substitute. It is the lack of the correct foods that will be responsible for any failure in breeding.

The species is rather aggressive and is really better in a tank by itself, but individuals will settle down in a communal tank providing the other members are somewhat similar in size.

For breeding, the tank should be planted according to the standard description and the temperature raised to 75°F. Spawn is deposited either in shallow depressions in the sand, or among the plant roots, and hatches in about a week. Remove the female immediately after spawning, but do not disturb the male, who will protect the eggs (he will do this even from the female) and guard the young when they are born.

It is a beautiful and interesting fish with a preference for alkaline water.

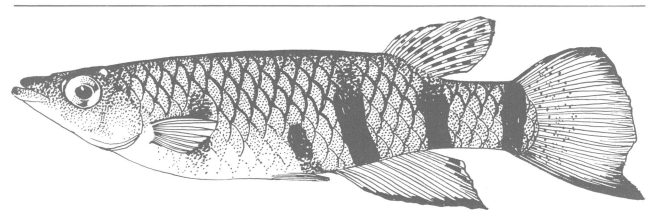

Name	Playfairs panchax
Scientific name	*Pachypanchax playfairii*
Average temperature	75°F
Community	No
Breeding	Page 55
Reproduction	Oviparous
Natural location	Zanzibar, Seychelles, E. Africa

The body colour of the male is yellow to yellow-green. The female is similar in colour, but perhaps slightly more brown and lighter in tone. The body of the male is well marked with rows of red spots which extend into the dorsal, caudal and anal fins. The caudal and anal fins have a red and black edge. Fins of the male are brownish or yellow, and clear in the female except for a dark spot on her dorsal.

A most distinctive feature of this species is the protruding scales along the front dorsal surface of the body, these scales stand out from the body like the teeth of a saw.

It is not a good community fish as it is somewhat pugnacious and carnivorous, it will also try to leap out of its tank.

This species also seems to like a little salt in the water and one teaspoonful of sea-salt to each gallon of water is approximately the correct proportion.

Adult fish attain a length of 3½–4 in. They spawn at 75°F and will eat their own eggs and young, therefore the plants in the breeding tank must be dense and include floating plants, and the adults should be removed as soon as possible after spawning.

Characins

The Characins are generally hardy fish, and make excellent aquarium species, although few are easily bred.

As a rule they are quite peaceful, but sometimes a larger fish will nibble the fins of the smaller ones. Feeding presents no real problem as they take readily to dried foods, but they should be given a variety including live foods.

Although the Characins are tropical, they are not particularly fond of high temperatures—an average of 70°–74°F being about right.

They breed in the same manner as described for egg-laying tooth carps, but with a few exceptions which will be noted under individual headings. The eggs are adhesive or semi-adhesive, and in nearly all cases will be eaten by the parents if this is allowed. They make no effort to protect their young, in fact they appear to consider them as tit-bits.

The Characins belong to the super-order Ostariophysi, sub-order Characoidei, and are grouped under the family Characidae. They are closely related to the Cyprinids (carp-like fish with toothless and protractile mouths) but can be distinguished by a general rule that they have teeth in their mouth, and an adipose fin. Most Characins have both of these features, but some will only possess one. Rarely, if ever, will a Characin be found without either.

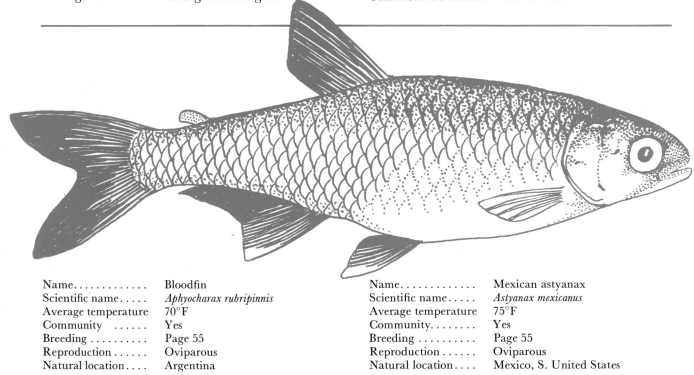

Name	Bloodfin
Scientific name	*Aphyocharax rubripinnis*
Average temperature	70°F
Community	Yes
Breeding	Page 55
Reproduction	Oviparous
Natural location	Argentina

Name	Mexican astyanax
Scientific name	*Astyanax mexicanus*
Average temperature	75°F
Community	Yes
Breeding	Page 55
Reproduction	Oviparous
Natural location	Mexico, S. United States

The bloodfin is a most pleasing fish, and it is shown to its best advantage when its silvery-green body is caught by a streak of daylight, which gives it a metallic sheen. The fins, as may be expected, are red. Bloodfins are easily fed, well behaved, and extremely active, which are all very desirable qualities.

Breeding is as in the standard description. The eggs are non-adhesive. Sexing is by means of a white tip to the ventral and anal fins of the male. The red in the fins is usually a slightly darker tint in the male also, but this is not a very reliable indication.

The breeding temperature should be 75°–80°F and these fish seem to have a preference for alkaline water.

This is not a particularly colourful aquarium fish. Its main charm lies in its hardiness, and the fact that it is one of the easiest Characins to breed.

It is a silvery fish, darkening to olive along the upper body; occasionally specimens are found that reflect very pale yellow from the body scales. A wide bluish band of colour extends from the upper edge of the gill covers to the base of the tail. It is marked with a dark sloping bar behind the head, and a dark spot at the root of the tail. Adult aquarium species will grow to about 3 in., their wild relatives to about 4 in.

Brachydanio abolineatus
Barbus ticto
Barbus tetrazona

These fish present no feeding problems, they will eat almost any food.

The Mexican astyanax breeds in the manner of most Characins, but it is particularly similar to *Hemigrammus caudovittatus*. *A. bimaculatus* is a similar species that is slightly larger, but it is not quite so easy to breed.

Name..............	Threadlike fish
Scientific name.....	*Copeina arnoldi*
Average temperature	73°F
Community........	Yes
Breeding..........	See below
Reproduction......	Oviparous
Natural location....	Amazon Basin, Brazil

In *Copeina arnoldi* we have a most unusual fish, unusual if only for its peculiar breeding habits.

Whilst not an outstanding fish with regard to colour, it has a rather nice body shape, and attractive fins. The main body colouring is an olive-brown, with darker markings on the scale edges and around the mouth. Both ventral and anal fins are a suffused red, and the same colour is also present on the lower fork of the caudal fin. The dorsal fin differs according to the sex; in the female it shows a red spot, but in the male there is a white spot contrasted by a dark spot immediately in front of it. Although this species is a member of the Characin family, there is no adipose fin.

Nature has provided many ingenious ways for the protection of her creatures when in the early stages of their existence. *Copeina arnoldi* is an example of the extremes to which a creature will go to ensure a measure of protection for safeguarding its offspring.

When he has found a suitable plant above the actual water surface, the male drives the female towards it, then they lock, or partially lock, their fins together and leap out of the water on to the plant leaf, where the eggs are deposited.

For aquarium breeding, put the pair of fish into a tank about 24 in. × 12 in. × 12 in. The water should be about 8-in. deep, and have a pH of 7 or slightly less. The temperature should be between 75° and 80°F. A piece of roughened glass or slate will substitute for the plant. Place this so that it projects above the water level, the rough surface will allow the eggs to adhere.

Cover the aquarium with a sheet of glass. The absence of a suitable sloping piece of material rising out of the water may result in the fish trying to deposit their eggs on the glass cover, from which they will fall back into the aquarium and become lost.

If the fish are in condition, the act of spawning

Rasbora heteromorpha

will take place as described above, the fish jumping about 2 in. out of the water. They adhere to the slate or glass for a few seconds during which from six to twelve eggs are laid and fertilised. The fish then fall back into the water. This operation is repeated until approximately 100 eggs are deposited. It is then advisable to remove the female. The male will tend the eggs, keeping them moist by splashing them periodically with water. This he does by swimming under the eggs and splashing with his tail, causing the water to spurt upwards. When not actually performing this operation, the male likes to hide, therefore it will be necessary to provide a plant thicket at one end of the aquarium. When the eggs hatch, usually in about three days, the fry drop into the water. Remove the male.

It is as well to feed the adult fish on live foods such as daphnia, chopped earthworm, and insect larvæ to get them in breeding condition.

Name............	Red spotted copeina
Scientific name.....	*Copeina guttata*
Average temperature	74°F
Community........	Yes
Breeding..........	See below
Reproduction......	Oviparous
Natural location....	Amazon Basin

Although not a particularly glamorous fish, *C. guttata* has the advantage that it is easy to breed and to raise the fry, so it is a good species for the novice to try his hand at breeding.

Body colour is grey-brown with a bluish sheen and the belly is very pale, almost white. The body is marked with red spots which form longitudinal rows, and the fins are yellow tinted. The edges of the anal, ventral, and caudal fins are orange to red.

Usually fish confined in an aquarium are smaller than those found in the wild, but with *C. guttata* the opposite is true. Aquarium specimens will grow to about 4 in., sometimes larger, whilst those from natural waters rarely exceed 3 in.

An aquarium about 12 in. × 12 in. × 24 in. is ideal for breeding, it should not be smaller. The pair of fish form a depression in the sand into which the eggs are deposited and fertilised. The male then assumes guardianship by driving the female away and fanning the eggs. The number of eggs are prodigious; any number up to a thousand may be deposited during one spawning, and these should hatch in 48 hours at a temperature of 75°F. The female should be removed immediately after spawning, and the male as soon as the young fish are free swimming.

These are hardy fish that have a wide temperature tolerance from 60° to 90°F and flourish well at the usual average aquarium temperature of 75°F.

Name............	Silver tetra
Scientific name.....	*Ctenobrycon spilurus*
Average temperature	70°F
Community........	Yes
Breeding	Page 55
Reproduction	Oviparous
Natural location....	Guiana

This is an old tropical favourite. It is not seen now so much, probably because it requires plenty of space.

It is not a particularly colourful fish. Its main attraction is the silvery mirror-like quality of the flat body which reflects subtle tints as it flashes about the aquarium. The only markings it can boast are two black spots, one behind the gill cover and the other at the tail root. The fins have a yellowish tint.

The silver tetra, when fully grown, attains a length of approximately 3 in., and it is very active. Whilst this feature does not exclude it from the community tank, it is not advisable to put it in with fish that would be disturbed by such activity. This fish feeds well on both dried and live foods and is quite happy in relatively low temperatures between 65° to 70°F.

When in breeding condition, the anal fin of the *female* becomes suffused with red. Another sex indication is the body size—mature females are usually slightly larger and deeper in body than the males.

Breeding is not difficult if the fish are in condition and a large tank, say 30 in., is used. Water should be at a depth of 10 in. and at a temperature of 75° to 80°F.

The addition of a glass partition between the pair will enable the aquarist to watch for signs of the breeding urge. The partition can then be removed. Last thing at night is the best time to do this. The eggs, usually about 200, adhere to the plants and hatch in two days.

Name............	Black widow
Scientific name.....	*Gymnocorymbus ternetzi*
Average temperature	70°F
Community........	Yes
Breeding	Page 55
Reproduction	Oviparous
Natural location....	Paraguay

The black widow is sometimes confused in name with the merry widow, although in appearance they are decidedly dissimilar.

The black widow is a smart fish, its dark colouring provides an excellent contrast to lighter coloured fish. The large anal fin is fan-shaped and black in hue. This colour suffuses the whole of the rear portion of the body up to and including the dorsal fin. Two or three vertical lines of black are also visible on the remainder of the body. The caudal fin is so translucent that it is sometimes difficult to see. Black widows up to about $1\frac{1}{8}$-in. long have the deepest colouring, but as they grow over this length the markings become paler until they are really a dark shade of grey. The average length of a fully grown fish is $2\frac{1}{2}$ in.

Sexing is best ascertained by selecting the females when they are obviously filled with spawn. They breed according to the standard description for egg-layers.

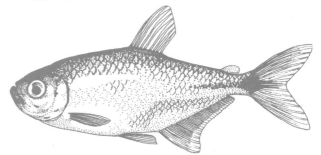

Name............	Buenos Aires tetra
Scientific name.....	*Hemigrammus caudovittatus*
Average temperature	75°F
Community........	Yes
Breeding	Page 55
Reproduction	Oviparous
Natural location....	La Plata Basin

This fish is one of the largest *Hemigrammus* in the aquarium world, growing to a length of approximately 3 in.

It is debatable if this fish should be included in the community tank because it has a tendency to nip the fins of other fish.

H. caudovittatus has a silvery body, and red fins. Unfortunately, after reaching a length of 2 in., the colouring becomes less brilliant and consequently the fish loses some of its attractiveness.

This species is easy to spawn. The tank should be fairly large, say 12 to 15 gallons. The male chases the female into the plant thickets, where she drops semi-adhesive eggs. Temperature for breeding should be in the region of 73°F.

The females are the more aggressive, sometimes chasing and even killing the male. This is not so during the actual spawning, however.

Generally, it is also easy to feed and quite hardy, enjoying a wide temperature range of 60°–80° F.

Astyanax mexicanus
Capeina arnoldi

Name............	Beacons or head and tail lights
Scientific name.....	*Hemigrammus ocellifer*
Average temperature	72°F
Community........	Yes
Breeding	Page 55
Reproduction......	Oviparous
Natural location....	British Guiana and Amazon

The 'beacons' or 'head and tail lights' are so named because the eye and top of the tail root reflect a bright orange, and look as if they are jewels worn for some special occasion. The body colouring is a pale greenish-brown, with an indistinct brown line running the length of the body. The males have a faint white mark in the centre of the anal fin. Breeding is by the standard method at a temperature of 76°F.

For Characins they are relatively easy to breed and are a good species for the new breeder.

Name............	Red nose tetra
Scientific name.....	*Hemigrammus rhodostomus*
Average temperature	76°F
Community........	Yes
Breeding	Page 55
Reproduction......	Oviparous
Natural location....	Amazon

Red nose tetras are peaceful but delicate fish that attain a length of about 1½ in. at maturity. The nose and forehead is deep red, and the body silvery tending to olive on the back with a light yellow on the belly. A dark stripe runs down the side of the body increasing in width as it extends

Ctenbrycon spilurus

into the tail. The tail has a dark angular mark on each lobe.

Spawning may be encouraged in soft water at a temperature of 80°F, and pH 6·8, otherwise it breeds in the standard manner.

The red nose tetra is not an easy species to breed although it may well be worth a try.

Name............	Feather fin
Scientific name.....	*Hemigrammus unilineatus*
Average temperature	75°F
Community........	Yes
Breeding	Page 55
Reproduction......	Oviparous
Natural location....	N.E. South America

The feather fin is easily recognised by the anal fin marking; this marking takes the form of a black and white line down the front edge. The caudal fin is faintly coloured a reddish-brown. The body is mainly silver.

This is a good fish for the community tank as it is peaceful and easy to feed. It is also quite a hardy fish, with a temperature range between 68° to 85°F. The breeding temperature is about 76°F.

Breeding is almost the same as for *Hyphessobrycon*

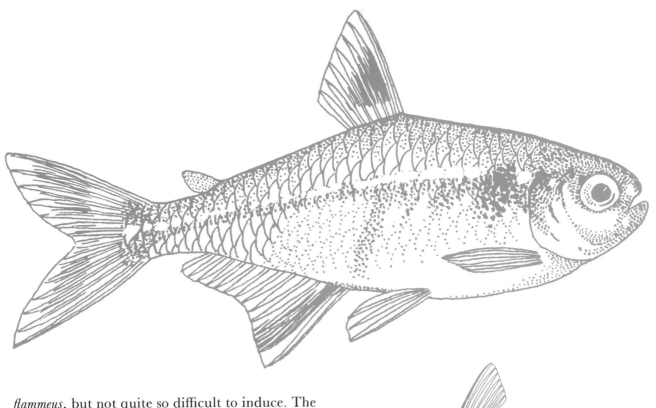

flammeus, but not quite so difficult to induce. The young, being slightly larger, do not require their initial foods so minute.

Name.............	Yellow tet
Scientific name.....	*Hyphessobrycon bifasciatus*
Average temperature	72°F
Community........	Yes
Breeding..........	Page 55
Reproduction......	Oviparous
Natural location....	S.E. Brazil

By comparison with some of the previous fish, the yellow tet is somewhat plain, but should not be ignored on that account.

The body colouring is silver-grey, overcast by a darkish yellow, which, when caught by a complementary angle of light, reflects a metallic iridescence. Just behind the head there are two vertical dark lines. It is an excellent community fish, growing to 2¼-in. long, and has the virtue of being comparatively easily bred, a fact which the beginner will appreciate.

Name.............	Dawn tetra
Scientific name.....	*Hyphessobrycon eos*
Average temperature	75°F
Community........	Yes
Breeding..........	Page 55
Reproduction......	Oviparous
Natural location....	British Guiana

The beauty of the dawn tetra is rather difficult to describe by words alone, the delicate colours of the body are variable and elusive under certain conditions. However, the colour of the body is

Gymnocorymbus ternetzi

generally a warm gold to a coppery-bronze, with an overtone of red or orange. The back is the same tone but darker, and the belly silvery white with a sheen not unlike mother-of-pearl. Numerous very small spots cover the entire body and have the effect of slightly darkening the general body colour.

The dawn tetra is not very decisively marked, it has a faint spot on the shoulder, a lateral stripe and a well defined dark spot on the lower part of the tail root. The gill covers reflect a beautiful flash of metallic blue-green. Fins are mainly tinted a golden yellow, and the lower lobe of the tail is somewhat darker than the upper lobe. The base of the tail fin is red.

As usual, the male is the more brilliantly coloured of the sexes, he is also smaller and slimmer than the female. The adult fish average about 1¾ in. in length.

The dawn tetra breeds in the same way as other small Characins and, although it is not too easy to breed, it has on occasions been successfully accomplished.

It may be of interest to know that the meaning of the word *eos* is Greek goddess of the dawn, from its rosy colour.

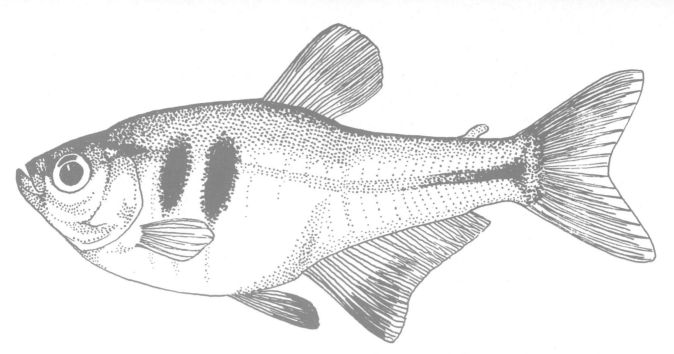

Name.............	Flame fish
Scientific name......	*Hyphessobrycon flammeus*
Average temperature	70°F
Community........	Yes
Breeding..........	Page 55
Reproduction......	Oviparous
Natural location....	Rio de Janeiro

The 'tet from Rio' is only 1½ in. in length but has such a delicate beauty that it is in continual demand. The body colouring is silver with a decided flush of pink deepening in density, as it approaches the tail, into a delicate rose red which entirely covers the anal fin and gives rise to the name 'flammeus,' meaning flame-like. The adipose fin is apparent as with most Characins, but it is quite small. Given plenty of room and fed well with occasional variations of daphnia, the 'tet' will show itself to advantage.

Sexing can be done by several methods. The males have the typical hook to the anal fin. The hook is situated on the rear end of the anal fin, but it is extremely difficult to see it with the naked eye. For this reason you should be careful when netting, as the anal fin tends to become caught in the mesh of the net. The anal fin is also fuller in the male.

They breed almost in the standard manner. A thick clump of *Myriophyllum* or similar fine-leafed plant should be placed in one end of the aquarium. The courtship consists of lively chasing by the male, which ends in the pair lying in a parallel position among the plants. About ten eggs are then dropped and fertilised. This is repeated until a hundred eggs or more have been dropped. These small, translucent, slightly adhesive eggs will remain among the plants if not disturbed. Those which fall off have about a fifty-fifty chance of hatching. A higher percentage of fertilised eggs

can be expected if two males are used to one female. Immediately upon completion of the spawning, the tetras should be removed, for it is then that they are most likely to eat the eggs.

Most fish prefer live daphnia to their own eggs, so a *small* quantity should be given whilst the spawning is taking place.

Greenwater is a good first food, followed by infusoria or egg water.

Name.............	Flag tetra
Scientific name.....	*Hyphessobrycon heterorhabdus*
Average temperature	75°F
Community........	Yes (but keep with fish of similar size)
Breeding..........	Page 55 and below
Reproduction......	Oviparous
Natural location....	Amazon

a dark background and a good top light, and preferably a tank solely devoted to a number of specimens. However, space does not always permit this luxury, but do try and keep them with fish no larger than themselves.

The males have a hook on the anal fin, so sexing is relatively easy, but breeding them is not. If, however, you feel inclined to try, use the method

This species is also known as the striped Characin, and the Belgium flag fish. It is a showy and beautiful fish, but like most jewels it requires the correct setting.

The body is silvery, but reflects a translucent green, and it is marked with a horizontal stripe of yellow, bordered above by red and below by a blue-black line—hence the reference to the Belgium flag. This line extends from just behind the gill covers to the tail root. The fins are usually clear, or very pale straw colour. To show these fish to their best advantage it is necessary to have

Hyphessobrycon bifasciatus

described for *H. flammeus*. Adults attain a length of about 2 in. *Hemigrammus ulreyi* is a similar species, but it lacks the brilliance of colour.

Name............	Neon tetra
Scientific name.....	*Hyphessobrycon innesi*
Average temperature	72°F
Community........	Yes (if not placed with large fish)
Breeding	See below
Reproduction	Oviparous
Natural location....	Amazon

The neon tetra is generally regarded as the most beautiful of all aquarium fish, and rightly deserves this honour. Even colour photography cannot capture the neon-like fluorescence given off by a vivid streak of bluish green running from the eye to the tail, with a dark olive green border on the top and below. A nicely planted aquarium with about twenty of this species is an unforgettable sight.

It also has a red marking which has the pecularity of staining white paper when a dead specimen is laid upon it; this indicates that the colouring matter is a pigment, and accounts for its sustained brilliance when the fish is frightened or excited.

Unfortunately, very little is known about the neon tetras' breeding habits. They have been bred successfully in the aquarium, but not consistently, for the eggs tend to disappear in the water. W. T. Innes gives the following procedure in his *Exotic Aquarium Fishes*.

'As females show signs of filling with roe they are separated from the males, and when regarded as ripe a single pair is placed at night in a bare tank containing newly drawn water that has stood not over one day. As spawn is dropped on the bottom of the tank, the female tries to eat it, but the male drives her away. Eggs are lifted by dip tube and hatched in another container, bare except for a big flat stone raised about an inch. The newly hatched young, which are small and difficult to see, attach themselves by their noses to the underside of the stone. They are reared by the standard infusoria, brine shrimp, sifted daphnia schedule.'

Successful spawnings have been induced in America by the following procedure. Water with a pH value of 6·5–7 is used, and this pH should be checked once a week and corrected if necessary by the addition of sodium phosphate. This correction must, of course, be done gradually over a period of three to four days.

The water should also be very soft, approximately 50 parts/million, and made up of distilled water and tap water. It is an advantage to keep neons in this soft water even prior to breeding, and, if possible, actually raise them in it. Newly acquired specimens, even if not reared in it, should be transferred to soft water upon arrival.

Cleanliness is of great importance. The eggs are sometimes destroyed by bacteria which penetrate the protective membrane. Every precaution possible should be taken to ensure everything is spotless that enters the tank—nets, thermometer, plants, cover glass, etc., should be as near sterile as they can be made. This reduces the possibility of bacteria entering and perhaps destroying the eggs of an otherwise successful spawning. A small tank, about three gallons capacity, has an advantage over larger ones. This should be planted with a bunch of fine-leafed plants that have first been sterilised by putting them in water containing one tablespoonful of powdered alum per two quarts for ten minutes.

Introduce the fish into the tank during the evening, first sterilising them by putting them into a separate tank of water to which one teaspoonful of sea salt per gallon and enough permanganate of potash to turn the water pink has been added. Leave them in this solution for ten minutes. It is important to ensure that this solution is at the same temperature, pH, and softness as the breeding tank.

The fish, if in breeding condition, should begin to spawn the next morning. If they do not spawn during that day, remove about one half of the water and replace with fresh distilled water, slightly cooler. After a successful spawning, the tank should be blacked out for a period of five days.

The eggs hatch in approximately 24 hours and vary in number between 15 to 100. Remove the parents immediately after spawning, and return them to their own tank via the sterilising tank. Whilst the adult fish are in the breeding tank, they can be fed on half-grown brine shrimps. Still keeping in mind the necessity for cleanliness, rinse them for ten minutes in a solution of water and rock salt, two tablespoons of salt to two ounces of water. Finally, rinse them in clean tap water before transferring them into the breeding tank.

Start feeding the fry on the fifth day. It is fatal to feed them on infusoria. Use instead hard-boiled egg yolk squeezed through a piece of fine muslin and mixed with distilled water. This mix should be sterilised by boiling for ten minutes in a stoppered bottle. The stopper must have a small hole in it to prevent it exploding. Feed twice daily approximately one drop for every ten fry. Warning— make sure the egg infusion is always fresh, it will keep in a refrigerator up to a week. Frygrain should be fed on the eighth day. This food is light and will float on the surface where the fry are

Hyphessobrycon heterorhabdus

Hyphessobrycon innesi

now swimming.

After two weeks the fry can be fed newly hatched brine shrimps. At the same time, the tank should be gradually lightened by removing a portion of the covering. The complete lightening of the tank should be over a period of about a week.

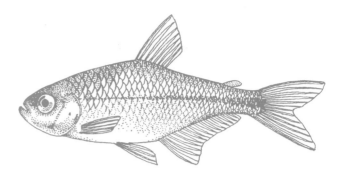

Name............	Dwarf tetra
Scientific name.....	*Hyphessobrycon minimus*
Average temperature	75°F
Community........	Yes (if not with large fish)
Breeding	Not known
Reproduction......	Oviparous
Natural location....	Guiana, Amazon Basin

The dwarf tetra, as may be expected, is one of the smaller species of fish suitable for aquaria. Adult specimens rarely grow any larger than ¾ in.

Body colour is yellow-green to silver-grey, marked on the side with a dark line, which is underlined by a blue metallic line starting from the gill covers and terminating in a round dark spot at the base of the tail fin. The fins are hyaline and both the dorsal and anal fins are marked with a dark line at the base. The tail fin has a faint blue blush near the root, and is slightly smokey at the tips.

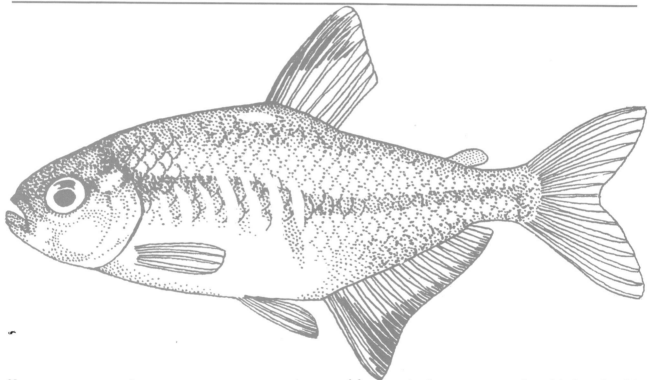

Name............	Lemon tetra
Scientific name.....	*Hyphessobrycon pulchripinnis*
Average temperature	73°F
Community........	Yes
Breeding	See page 55 and below
Reproduction......	Oviparous
Natural location....	Amazon Basin

The general body colour of this typical tetra is yellow. The first rays of the anal fin are coloured a slightly deeper yellow, followed immediately by an intense black stripe; the bottom edge of this fin is also black streaked, and the front rays of the dorsal fin are black also. The upper half of the eye is vivid red, and the lower half is yellow.

These fish have been bred successfully in captivity, but they are not easily induced to spawn, neither are the fry easy to rear, but this fact should not prevent the enthusiastic aquarist from trying his hand.

In general, the instructions for breeding given for *H. innesi* apply equally well for *H. pulchripinnis*. The water depth should be about 3 in., and slightly alkaline (pH 7·2–7·4). Rain water or distilled water mixed with tap water is necessary for breeding this species. The plants should be fine leafed, well cleaned, and left free floating in fairly dense clusters.

Do not use any sand on the floor of the aquarium. Strong artificial or direct natural lighting is harmful to ova and fry up to two weeks old. Therefore, ensure that only a subdued top light is used during this period. The breeding temperature is 80°F.

84

Name..............	Rosy tetra
Scientific name.....	*Hyphessobrycon rosaceus*
Average temperature	76° F
Community........	Yes
Breeding..........	Oviparous
Reproduction......	Page 55 and below
Natural location....	Guiana and Brazil

Although the beautiful rose pink of the body is enough to make this tetra an aquarium favourite, its appeal is further enhanced by a high black dorsal fin edged along the front by a white margin. All other fins are flushed pink, and the ventral and anal fins are often white tipped.

Sexing adult fish is not difficult, the male has the larger and more pointed dorsal fin. The dorsal of the female usually has a brighter red tip. The average size of adults is about 1¾ in.

The rosy tetra is not an easy species to breed. The aquarium must be very clean, and filled to about 8-in. deep with fresh, but matured, tap water. Anchor plants to leave a clear area just below the surface as it is likely that spawning will occur above the plants. The temperature should be raised to 80° F. In all other respects this species breed in exactly the same manner as does *H. flammeus*.

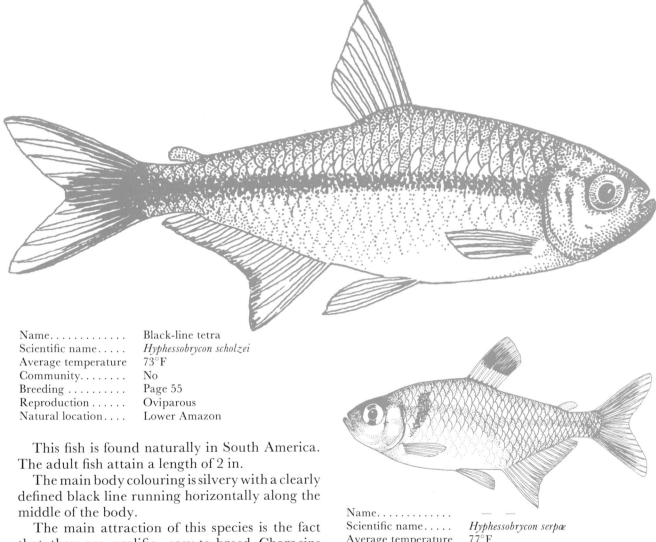

Name..............	Black-line tetra
Scientific name.....	*Hyphessobrycon scholzei*
Average temperature	73° F
Community........	No
Breeding..........	Page 55
Reproduction......	Oviparous
Natural location....	Lower Amazon

This fish is found naturally in South America. The adult fish attain a length of 2 in.

The main body colouring is silvery with a clearly defined black line running horizontally along the middle of the body.

The main attraction of this species is the fact that they are prolific, easy-to-breed Characins which are well suited as a beginner's fish. The eggs, which are deposited on fine-leafed plants, are adhesive. The normal temperature range is between 65°–80° F, but this should be adjusted to about 78° F for breeding purposes.

Black-line tetras are bad fish to put indiscriminately into a community tank, as they have a tendency to chase other fish and devour any small enough to be eaten.

Name..............	
Scientific name.....	*Hyphessobrycon serpæ*
Average temperature	77°F
Community........	Yes
Breeding..........	See *H. flammeus*
Reproduction......	Oviparous
Natural location....	Brazil

This pretty little fish is found naturally in Brazil, and grows to a length of approximately 1½ in., sometimes slightly larger. It also has the virtue of a quiet and peaceful disposition.

The body has a strong red colouring which

continues into the fins. Opaque white edgings to the fins give this fish an outstanding and somewhat striking appearance. This is further emphasised by the black edging to the anal fin.

It breeds in a similar manner to that described for *Hyphessobrycon flammeus*. The normal temperature range is 70°–85°F.

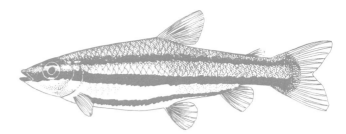

Name	— —
Scientific name	*Nannostomus trifasciatus*
Average temperature	75°F
Community	Yes (do not overcrowd)
Breeding	Page 55 and below
Reproduction	Oviparous
Natural location	Amazon

N. trifasciatus is a fish which is ideally suited to life in an aquarium. It is pretty, peaceful, hardy and grows to an ideal size, averaging about 1¾-in. long.

A black line extends from the lower lip to the tail root, and the belly below this line is white with a very thin broken line following the lower body contour. Above the thick line, a wide golden stripe runs down the body with a thin black line about it. Adult fish have all fins, except pectorals, marked with a red spot. Red spots are also present in the golden stripe of the male. The adiposa fin is generally present but may be lacking.

Spawning is not too easy, but it has been accomplished. *Riccia* and a few submerged plants should be placed in the breeding tank. The eggs are adhesive, and hatch in two to three days at a temperature of 75°F. The fry become adults in seven months.

Parents are unlikely to eat the eggs unless they are hungry, but remove them just to be sure.

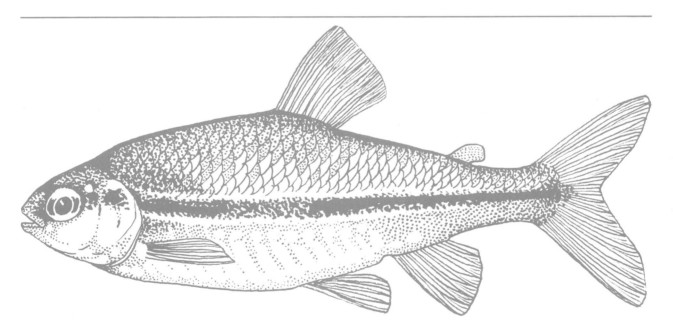

Name	African tetra
Scientific name	*Nannæthiops unitæniatus*
Average temperature	73°F
Community	Yes
Breeding	Page 55
Reproduction	Oviparous
Natural location	Nile, Niger, Congo, Gold Coast

Africa invariably suggests tropical animals large and small but it is surprising how few fish for the aquarium actually come from there. One of these, however, is the African tetra. The body of this fish, unlike most Characins, is more rounded. The upper portion of the body is a brownish-red,

Hyphessobrycon rosaceus

golden on the sides, merging into pale yellow to white on the lower body and the underparts. The dark lateral marking has a gold line above it which tends to become coppery as it approaches the tail. This coppery colour extends into the top half of the caudal fin, spreading out into a reddish suffusion. The lower half is also suffused with red but is not as bright as the top. The fore edge of the dorsal fin is black, and there is sometimes red present in this fin also. The scales are clearly defined as they are usually finely edged with black.

The African tetra is decidedly an attractive fish, quite peaceful, hardy and easy to feed. It will thrive on dried foods, but live foods should be included in the diet.

Mature females attain a length of approximately 3 in.; the males are slightly smaller, about 2½ in.

Breeding is reasonably easy to induce; the temperature should be raised to between 78° and 82°F.

The breeding aquarium should be spacious and planted with fine-leafed plants. Eggs hatch in about two days. After three to four days they should be fed fine live foods.

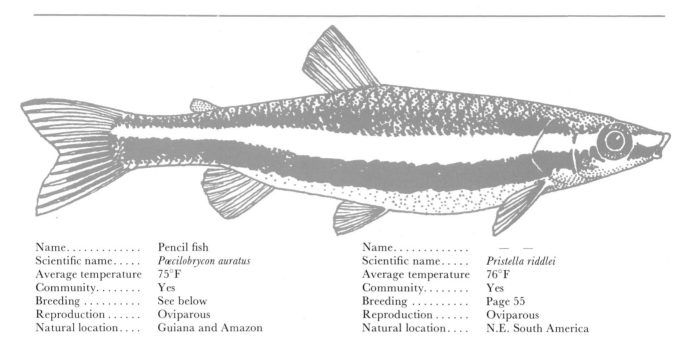

Name............	Pencil fish
Scientific name.....	*Pœcilobrycon auratus*
Average temperature	75°F
Community........	Yes
Breeding	See below
Reproduction	Oviparous
Natural location....	Guiana and Amazon

Name............	— —
Scientific name.....	*Pristella riddlei*
Average temperature	76°F
Community........	Yes
Breeding	Page 55
Reproduction	Oviparous
Natural location....	N.E. South America

This fish is generally a slow swimmer and it adopts an attitude of approximately 45°, with tail down, when swimming and at rest. The body colour is brown-grey, which changes to a golden brown along the back. It is marked with a light brownish stripe from the mouth to the upper lobe of the tail. A second stripe merges with the first at the base of the tail.

A much darker and wider stripe runs from the mouth, through the bottom half of the eye, and ends in the lower lobe of the tail, where it spreads to colour the entire area. A yellow stripe borders this broad stripe on top and extends from the upper jaw, through the eye and well into the upper lobe of the tail. The anal fin is brown and is marked with a red spot adjacent to the body. In the males the anal fin is convex; in females it is straight. The average length of adults is 2 in.

The pencil fish is relatively hardy and peaceful. It is, however, not a very easy species to spawn, so far attempts to spawn them in aquaria have not been very successful, although it is believed that they will spawn on the underside of *Sagittaria* leaves at a temperature of 82°F.

The number of eggs will be about 40, scattered singly among the leaves and they will hatch in about two days. Soft and slightly acid water is necessary.

The parents have a tendency to guard the eggs and should preferably be removed immediately the spawning is complete.

The *P. riddlei* was first imported into Europe in 1924 and this quick-moving exotic fish has been highly regarded by aquarists ever since. The females are about 1¾-in. long when fully grown, and the males are slightly smaller.

The ground colour of the body is silvery-grey with a soft brownish sheen, and it is almost transparent. Other characteristic markings are a dark spot just behind the gill covers, black and white patches on the dorsal and anal fins, and slightly lighter patches on the ventral fins. The base of the dorsal is lemon yellow, and ends in a white point. The streamlined forked tail has a reddish tint.

Sexes can be decided as for *H. flammeus*. A further indication is the dark area seen in the transparent belly. In the male this area is rather pointed, whilst in the female it is more rounded.

It is important to have a well matched pair, if successful breeding is to be obtained. Breeding is more or less standard, but courtship is slightly different. Spawning usually takes place in the early hours of the morning. They press together and swim in a circular motion to the surface, where the eggs are dropped over the plants. In two or three hours as many as two to three hundred eggs are deposited. Immediately after spawning the parents should be removed.

The eggs hatch within two days. The fry are

Tanichthys albonubes
Brachydanio rerio
Danio malabaricus

88

visible, looking like tiny glass splinters on the plants, and the sides and bottom of the tank. Early feeding must be with pond infusoria, as the home-cultured is much too big for their mouths. They can be nursed through the first ten days on this feed, then they are big enough to take micro-worms.

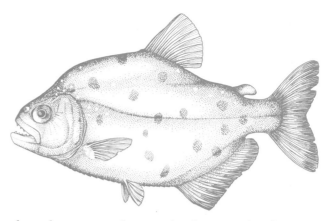

Name............	Piranha (spotted)
Scientific name.....	*Serrasalmus rhombeus*
Average temperature	75°F
Community........	No
Breeding..........	Not yet bred
Reproduction......	Oviparous
Natural location....	Amazon and Guiana

The piranha can hardly be described as a fish for the average aquarist. It is a ferocious blood-thirsty cannibal that must be housed in a large aquarium of its own. Having taken care of the accommodation, it must still be handled carefully, small specimens will give a finger quite a nip and larger ones can actually remove a piece of flesh.

In their natural waters, the piranha shoals are justly feared. It only needs the taste of blood to set the shoal into a mad frenzy of attack. So fierce is the attack, and numerous the shoal, that it is said that they can reduce quite large animals to a skeleton within minutes. The piranha is well equipped with razor-sharp, wedge-shaped teeth that cut into flesh fast and cleanly.

S. rhombeus is one of the two species available to the aquarist. It has a silvery body with a grey-green sheen, sprinkled with many dark spots. The anal and caudal fins are dark.

The other species *S. spilopleura* has a dark greyish-brown body peppered with silver spots, and a dark band through the eye to the gill cover.

Neither of these species has been bred in captivity.

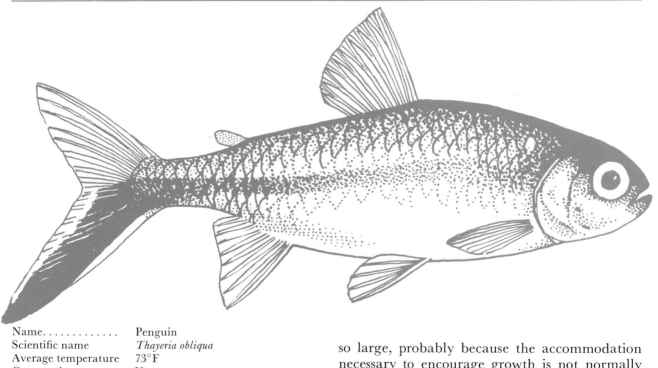

Name............	Penguin
Scientific name	*Thayeria obliqua*
Average temperature	73°F
Community........	Yes
Breeding..........	Page 55
Reproduction......	Oviparous
Natural location....	Amazon Basin

This is a really interesting fish. It comes from the Amazon Basin, and grows to a length of approximately 3½ in. I have never had one quite

Betta splendens

so large, probably because the accommodation necessary to encourage growth is not normally available.

The fish swims in the usual horizontal position, but assumes an oblique position when at rest, the head being higher than the tail.

The body colouring is silver, graduating into an olive on the back. A decisive black line runs from behind the gill covers along the centre of the body and into the lower fork of the tail. This line is edged by a thin iridescent stripe.

91

It breeds in the standard manner in an average temperature of 73°F. The eggs hatch in about two days. The tiny fry require microscopic live foods, initially. Green water is a good first food.

Hatchet fish

This family of fish is closely related to the Characidae and belongs to the super-order Ostariophysi, sub-order Characoidei and is grouped under the family Gasteropelecidae which represents the hatchet fish, or flying Characins. These fish are known as hatchet fish because they have a body shape resembling the blade of an axe, or hatchet—very slim, when viewed from the front, and very deep when viewed from the side.

There are three genera in the family, and in all three the species have well developed pectoral fins, not unlike wings, which are used by the fish to skim the water surface, and even to become airborne.

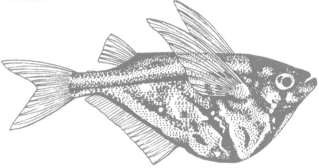

Name	Marbled hatchet fish
Scientific name	*Carnegiella strigata*
Average temperature	75° F
Community	Yes
Breeding	See below
Reproduction	Oviparous
Natural location	Guianas, Amazon

The body shape is similar to *Gasteropelecus levis*, but the fish are a little smaller. The average size attained by adults is about 1¾ in.

The body is silver, darkening to olive on the back, and overlaid with a dark 'marbling' pattern. These markings run diagonally forward across the fish from below the dorsal fin.

The marbled hatchet fish have been bred in captivity. They require a temperature in the region of 83°F and plenty of floating plants, such as duckweed and *Riccia*. The adhesive eggs are scattered among the plants. Sexing is difficult, there are no obvious differences except that the female has a wider body.

This species will consume dry foods, but live foods should be given frequently.

Pristella riddlei

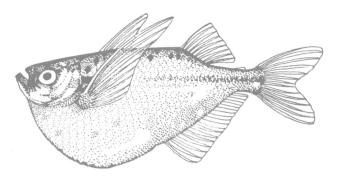

Name	Hatchet fish
Scientific name	*Gasteropelecus levis*
Average temperature	75°F
Community	Yes
Breeding	See below
Reproduction	Oviparous
Natural location	Guiana, Amazon Basin

The body of this species is shiny silver, darkening to an olive along the back. It is marked by two narrow stripes—one extending along the length of the body from the gill cover to the root of the tail, the other edges the body along the base of the anal fin. The fins are hyaline.

The pectoral fins are well developed into wing-like appendages, which enable the fish to skim the water surface and virtually 'take off' on a short flight. When viewed from the side, the belly is exceedingly deep, yet head-on they are very thin creatures. Adults attain a length of 2¼ in.

Hatchet fish are not bottom feeders, but they will accept food floating on or near the surface. They are carnivorous, and should not be given dried foods.

Although interesting little creatures, they do not live very long and, to the best knowledge of the author, have not been bred successfully in aquaria.

Carps and minnows

Carps and minnows belong to the super-order Ostariophysi, sub-order Cyprinoidei and are grouped under the family Cyprinidae (carp-like fish with toothless and protractile mouths). Instead of teeth in the jaw, these fish have curved pharyngeal bones in the throat which carry grinding teeth. A great number of carps have barbels—generally a maximum of two pairs, although there are a few species with more.

Name	Rosy barb
Scientific name	*Barbus conchonius*
Average temperature	70°F
Community	Yes
Breeding	Page 55
Reproduction	Oviparous
Natural location	India

One of the hardiest of the barbs, the rosy barb has the typical large mirror-like scales which are doubly enhanced at breeding time. The body of the male develops a flush of bronze, which makes him a handsome fellow indeed.

Other characteristic markings of the rosy barb are a black spot near the tail edged with pale orange, and slightly dark edging to the ventral and anal fins. The flush of colour is very volatile, and almost visibly melts away after spawning.

A fully grown rosy barb reaches a length of $3\frac{1}{2}$ in. The male is usually slightly smaller than the female. Sexing is easy at breeding time because of the colour of the male and the fuller body of the female.

The rosy barb breeds at a temperature of 80°F according to the standard description.

Name	Clown barb
Scientific name	*Barbus everetti*
Average temperature	75°F
Community	Yes
Breeding	Page 55
Reproduction	Oviparous
Natural location	Borneo and Malay peninsula

This is one of the larger barbs which attains a length of 4–5 in. It is a very attractive species with a yellow-pink body marked with several blue-grey blotches and triangular patches. The fins have a decided reddish hue.

Sexes can be determined by the more striking colour of the male, and the deeper body of the female. They spawn in the same manner as other barbs, but they do not breed readily, in fact they are most difficult. It is important to use a large aquarium, and provide artificial aeration—raise the temperature to about 80°F, and condition first for a few weeks by separating the sexes and feeding live foods.

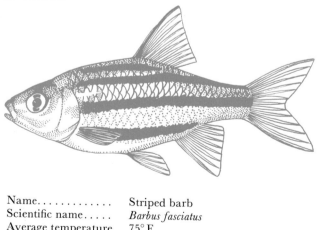

Name	Striped barb
Scientific name	*Barbus fasciatus*
Average temperature	75°F
Community	Yes
Breeding	Page 55 and below
Reproduction	Oviparous
Natural location	Borneo and Malaysia

This is one of the larger barbs and the adults can attain a length of 5 in. Its body is silvery, marked with four dark blue to black lateral stripes extending from just behind the gill covers to the tail root.

The female is similarly marked, but less well defined, and the stripes on her body are a little wider than the male's. They have two pairs of barbels.

Spawning *B. fasciatus* is difficult. The water should be soft and preferably slightly acid and at a temperature of 77–79° F.

Name	— —
Scientific name	*Barbus hexazona*
Average temperature	75°F
Community	Yes
Breeding	Page 55
Reproduction	Oviparous
Natural location	Malaysia and S.E. Asia

The body colour of *B. hexazona* is a pale yellow-brown, and is marked with six vertical dark bars. The bars commence with a line running through the eye and are more or less evenly spaced along the side of the body. The last bars are situated on the tail root and form a 'V', the base of which points forward.

It is only when the fish become adult that they are seen at their best, then the anal and dorsal fins of the male become suffused with red, and occasionally a few specks of red can be seen on the upper half of the body.

This is a peaceful fish that will grow to about $2\frac{1}{2}$ in. and will breed in the usual manner of barbs.

Name	Spanner barb
Scientific name	*Barbus lateristriga*
Average temperature	75°F
Community	No
Breeding	Page 55
Reproduction	Oviparous
Natural location	Malaya and East Indies

The spanner barb, when fully grown, attains a length of approximately $4\frac{1}{2}$–6 in., and it is mainly this large size that prevents it being included in the community category. They are, however, quite peaceful fish, but require large aquaria to house them.

The markings consist of two vertical bars, one just behind the gill cover and forward of the dorsal fin, the other below the forward end of the dorsal, into which the colouring extends. A lateral line extends from the fork of the caudal fin to just below the rear of the dorsal. There are also four spots, two on the tail root, one on the back, just behind the dorsal, and one on the lower body near the forward edge of the anal fin. These dark mark-

Barbus conchonius
Barbus everetti

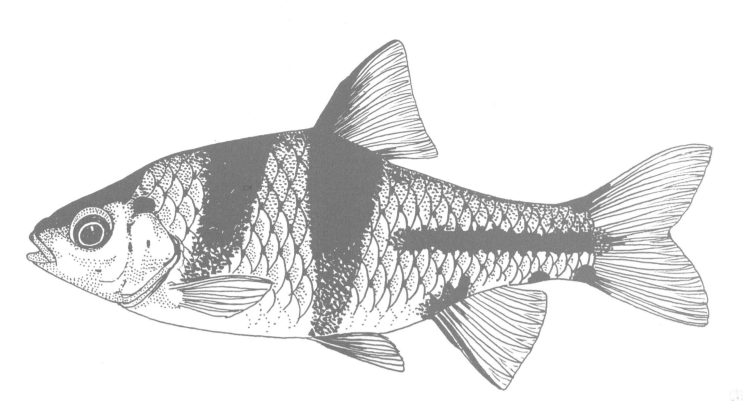

ings are on a body colour of pale gold and the fins are pinkish.

It is because of the position of the three main dark markings, which is representative of an adjusting spanner, that the spanner barb obtained its popular name.

These are not particularly colourful fish and when they increase their size even the black marking becomes less distinct. These fish were apparently first introduced to the aquarist in 1932.

This species does not like low temperatures; 70°F should be considered a minimum.

With regard to food, the spanner barb will eat the usual dried foods, but a diet of this nature will not be satisfactory by itself; plenty of live foods should be given to them. Favourite foods are daphnia and insect larvæ.

Sex differences are not easily found, but generally the male, when in breeding condition, has a more intense body colour, and the female a deeper body.

Breeding is not easy. Fish under 18 or 24 months should not be mated, but with fish over 24 months breeding can be attempted.

A partial change of water in the breeding tank may stimulate a spawning. The parents should be removed immediately after spawning, otherwise they will devour the eggs in record time. Many eggs are laid during a spawning, and hatch in about three days. The fry are able to eat food of micro-worm size in a very short time. Breeding temperature is 75°–80°F.

Barbus hexazona

Name............	Nigger barb or black ruby
Scientific name.....	*Barbus nigrofasciatus*
Average temperature	70°F
Community........	Yes
Breeding	Page 55
Reproduction	Oviparous
Natural location....	Ceylon

Like most of the barbs, *B. nigrofasciatus* has large, light-reflecting scales, and whilst it is not particularly brilliantly marked, it has sufficient virtues to warrant a place in any aquarium.

The main body colouring is greenish-yellow with cherry markings around the gill covers. The vertical bars are a sooty black which almost disappear when the fish are frightened or netted.

The most satisfactory way of sexing is to wait until the females fill with spawn, then segregate as previously described. The slightly better marking and blacker fins of the male can be used as an indication of sex.

When introduced to the female, the male blushes a cherry red from mouth to gill cover, and the remainder of its body becomes a suffused sooty black. It is a great pity that this breeding colour is not the everyday dress of this barb, as it would certainly make him one of the most handsome, but like most males he looks most handsome when he is courting.

This fish has an exceptionally good temper, and should be a welcome addition to any community tank.

The nigger barb is quite easily bred, and can be recommended for a first attempt at breeding egg-layers although it is not considered a productive species.

Name............	Checker barb
Scientific name.....	*Barbus oligolepis*
Average temperature	75°F
Community........	Yes
Breeding	Page 55
Reproduction	Oviparous
Natural location....	Sumatra

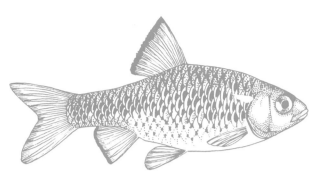

This is a truly beautiful fish, in fact this species is known as the 'beautiful barb' to American aquarists. The male is brilliantly coloured red-brown which darkens along the back, and lightens to silver along the underside. The scales along the lateral line are marked with blue-black spots, forming a checkered pattern. The fins are a particularly beautiful orange colour, and the dorsal fin is further enhanced with a thin black line edging the upper margin. This dorsal is very individualistic, no other barb can boast of such a feature.

When breeding, the male becomes even more beautiful, the dorsal fin deepens in colour and the body suffuses with black, through which the scales reflect blue and green.

Colouring in the female is similar to that of the male, but not so striking, also the fins are either only slightly tinted orange or hyaline. When adult the fish only average a little under 2-in. long.

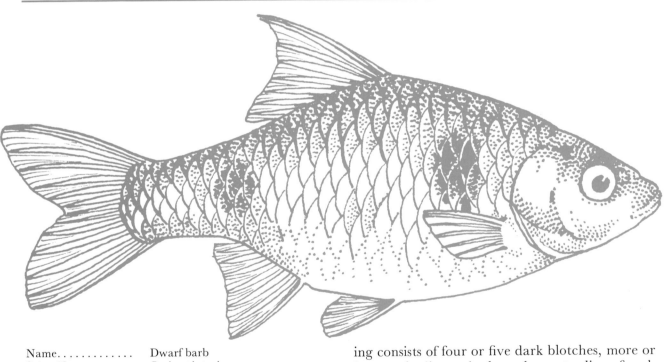

Name............	Dwarf barb
Scientific name.....	*Barbus phutunio*
Average temperature	75° F
Community........	Yes
Breeding	Page 55 and below
Reproduction	Oviparous
Natural location....	India

These small barbs are not a particularly brilliantly attractive species, but the adults attain a length of 1¼ in. and have beautiful fishy silver-blue scales that sparkle with reflected light. The marking consists of four or five dark blotches, more or less evenly disposed, along the centre line of each side. Pectoral fins are clear, all other fins have an orange or yellow tint. They do not have barbels. It is a peaceful and hardy community fish, but because of its small size it is not advisable for it to be included in aquaria containing large specimens. They are much better if kept in communities of their own kind as they are not particularly fond of their own company.

They are not ready breeders, but they will spawn at a temperature of 75° F.

Barbus nigrofasciatus

99

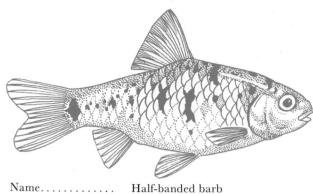

Name...........	Half-banded barb
Scientific name.....	*Barbus semifasciolatus*
Average temperature	75°F
Community.......	Yes
Breeding..........	Page 55
Reproduction......	Oviparous
Natural location....	South China

B. semifasciolatus is one of the less showy tropical fish, however it has other virtues. It is extremely hardy, it can withstand a temperature drop down to about 64°F, and it is easily bred.

General body colour is pale olive green, varying to a light orange-brown. It is marked with five or six vertical broken black bands on the upper half of the body. The fins are tinted pink or yellow. When ready to mate, the body of the male blushes red, and the fin coloration becomes more intense. Adult females attain a length of $2\frac{1}{2}$ in., and the males are a little smaller.

This species are quite prolific and their young grow quickly.

B. schuberti is a golden mutation of *B. semifasciolatus*.

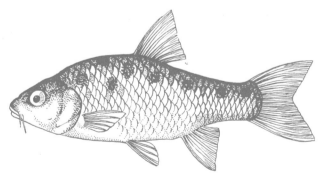

Name...........	Algerian barb
Scientific name.....	*Barbus setivimensis*
Average temperature	70°F
Community.......	Yes
Breeding..........	Page 55 and below
Reproduction......	Oviparous
Natural location....	North Africa

The body colour is silvery, lightening to white on the belly, and darkening to a beautiful coppery brown or olive brown along the back. It has two pairs of barbels. It is not a very striking fish, and

has one big disadvantage—it will grow to about 12-in. long.

Little is known about its breeding habits but you could assume initially that they breed like the majority of other barbs.

Name...........	One spot barb
Scientific name.....	*Barbus terio*
Average temperature	75°F
Community.......	Yes
Breeding..........	Page 55
Reproduction......	Oviparous
Natural location....	Bengal, Punjab, Orissa

Barbus terio is a similar species to *B. conchonius* but it has several different features that help to identify it. It grows only to about $2\frac{1}{2}$-in. long and, unlike *B. conchonius*, it is not so easy to breed.

The general body colour of the male is a bronze-yellow, it has a spot on its side, positioned above the anal fin, and another spot at the root of the tail. An indefinite line links these two spots together. There is also a reddish spot on the gill covers, and the fins are tinted orange. The female's body is silver and has hyaline fins.

At breeding time, the body of the male becomes a beautiful orange.

Name...........	Tiger barb
Scientific name.....	*Barbus tetrazona*
Average temperature	75°F
Community.......	Yes
Breeding..........	Page 55
Reproduction......	Oviparous
Natural location....	Malay peninsula, Borneo

The tiger barb is a very active, clearly defined fish. The general colouring of yellow is striped with four definite bands of black, one of which passes through the eye. On a good specimen, the dorsal fin has a dark base variegating through red to faint lemon. The ventral fin is red and the edges of the tail are also streaked with red.

The average length of the fully grown tiger barb is 2 in. Unfortunately, when they are about 1-in. long they seem to reach a critical stage, and are

Barbus tetrazana

likely to be delicate. Once this stage is past, how-ever, they are reasonably hardy.

The most reliable method of sexing is by the fuller body of the female, judged near breeding time.

Breeding temperature is around 85°F, and the procedure is the same as spawning the egg-layers. Remember they like eating their own eggs, so plant thickly and remove the parents immediately after spawning.

Tiger barbs present themselves best in an aquarium when about 40 of them are shown in a school.

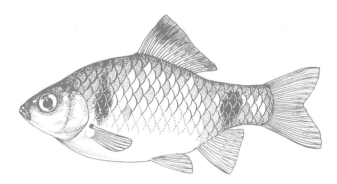

Name	— —
Scientific name	*Barbus ticto*
Average temperature	70°F
Community	Yes
Breeding	Page 55
Reproduction	Oviparous
Natural location	India

The *Barbus ticto* is not a particularly brilliantly marked fish, but it is of sufficient distinction to be included here.

The species is easily recognised by the red edging of the male's dorsal fin, which becomes particularly brilliant during the breeding period.

This red edging is also present on the female, but it is generally so faint as to be non-existent. It is, however, a little more noticeable at breeding time.

Body colouring is mainly silver with a hint of yellow, and there is a vertical dark bar just behind the gill cover, the only other marking is a dark spot on the body slightly behind the anal fin.

Although this is a barb they do not, in fact, have any barbels.

An average length for a fully grown adult is 3½ in. It is a very active species, continually frolicking around the aquarium. Its exuberance may be taken for aggressiveness as they nudge other fish in playfulness, but rarely do any real harm.

They are quite an easy fish to breed in the standard manner.

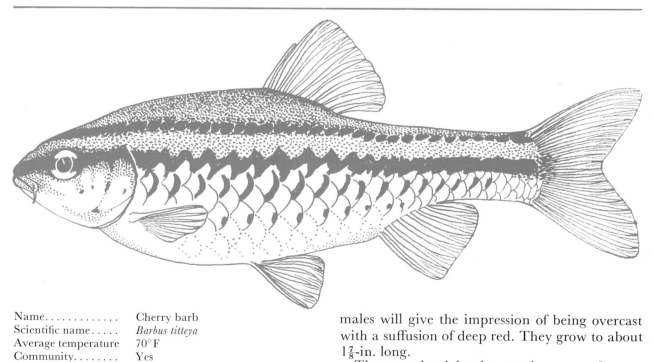

Name	Cherry barb
Scientific name	*Barbus titteya*
Average temperature	70°F
Community	Yes
Breeding	Page 55
Reproduction	Oviparous
Natural location	Ceylon

The cherry barbs are fish which are seen at their best when about forty of them are in a tank of their own. Their general colouring is a brownish-red with a blue-black lateral stripe. Occasionally, the

males will give the impression of being overcast with a suffusion of deep red. They grow to about 1⅞-in. long.

They are bred in the usual manner for egg bearers, but are avid egg eaters. They will not usually attempt to eat the eggs during an actual spawning, but will certainly do so afterwards if not removed.

They can be spawned in a tank devoid of sand. Anchor the plants by means of small pieces of lead. This method has the advantage of giving the aquarist the opportunity of seeing what is going on. The temperature of the water for breeding should be 78°F. The eggs hatch in about 36 hours.

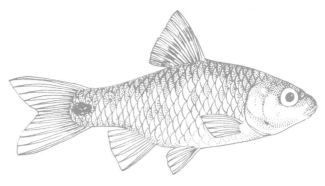

Name	
Scientific name	*Barbus vittatus*
Average temperature	70°F
Community	Yes
Breeding	Page 55
Reproduction	Oviparous
Natural location	Ceylon

B. vittatus is one of the smaller barbs and rarely exceeds 2-in. long. It is quiet, peaceful, and inoffensive, and it is rather surprising he is not more popular.

The body is silver with a black dot on the base of the tail, and the dorsal fin has a rusty-coloured base. All other fins are clear, and the iris of the eye is silver.

The meaning of the word *vittatus* is striped but it is difficult to find any stripes on this fish.

Breeding is according to the standard description—these fish are quite hardy and good breeders.

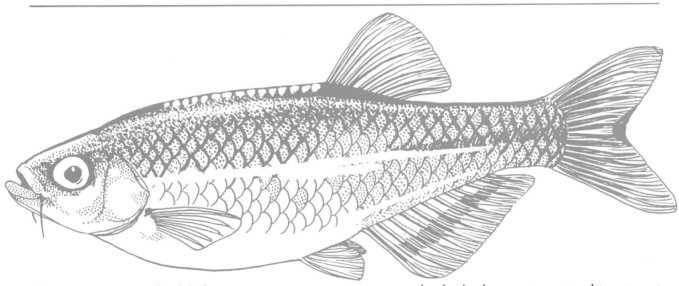

Name	Pearl danio
Scientific name	*Brachydanio abolineatus*
Average temperature	75°F
Community	Yes
Breeding	Page 55
Reproduction	Oviparous
Natural location	Burma

Like all danios, the 2½-in. *B. albolineatus* is full of energy, always flashing about in the tank as if full of the joys of living. The mother-of-pearl body scintillates with every twist of the body, reflecting delicate pastel shades of pink, blue and green, perfectly blended, and little hair-like barbels hang from the lower lip, which is characteristic of the carps.

Sexing is not easy at first glance, but with a little practice you will find it is not too difficult. The body of the female is deeper and slightly longer, and this becomes more noticeable as she fills with spawn.

When you are breeding pearl danios, the greatest difficulty is to prevent the eggs being eaten, as the danios have a strong tendency to eat their eggs as they fall. To prevent this the water should not be any deeper than 4 in., and a trap which prevents the parents from getting at the eggs should be installed. The trap can take the form of ¼-in. diameter glass marbles spread over the floor of the tank, and if no sand is used a glance up through the bottom of the tank will show you if a spawning has taken place. Marbles smaller than ¼-in. diameter should not be used, as frightened fish diving among them sometimes get wedged.

Another form of trap, preferable to marbles, is glass or Perspex bars wired together with soft lead wire to form a frame which you can raise about an inch off the bottom, and so leave plenty of room for inspection.

Sexes should be separated a week prior to breeding. Introduce the female a day before the male. A higher percentage of fertility will be maintained if three males are used to one female. If, however, the female seems to be worried by too

103

much attention, it is advisable to remove one male and leave only two.

The breeding temperature should be between 72°–77° F. The eggs are non-adhesive and hatch in two days, and the average number of eggs per spawning is 200.

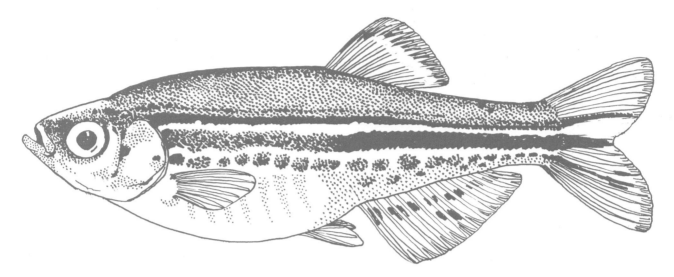

Name............	Spotted danio
Scientific name.....	*Brachydanio nigrofaciatus*
Average temperature	75°F
Community........	Yes
Breeding..........	Page 55
Reproduction......	Oviparous
Natural location....	Burma

This attractive danio is rather a small fish, which rarely exceeds 1½ in. The top half of the spotted danio is a shade of olive which grows paler as it descends down the body. The main stripe of Prussian blue extends the whole length of the body and across the tail, and below this is a row of blue spots.

The spotted danios are not bred so readily as the zebras, but the procedure is the same—the eggs being dropped during a partial embrace.

Name............	Zebra danio
Scientific name.....	*Brachydanio rerio*
Average temperature	75°F
Community........	Yes
Breeding..........	Page 55
Reproduction......	Oviparous
Natural location....	Bengal

The *B. rerio* or, as he is more commonly known, the 'zebra', grows to a length of approximately 1¾ in. when fully grown. The main body colouring is silvery white with clear-cut horizontal lines of deep blue which extend across the tail and anal fin. The zebra danio is a lively character who prefers to take his food from near the surface, but he will root around the bottom of the tank when hungry.

Sexing is best determined by the deeper body of the female, and bulging side when filled with roe.

Like all danios, the zebra is an extremely difficult fish to net. Two nets should always be used, otherwise you might lose patience and make a desperate bid, which may harm the fish.

The breeding procedure is as for *B. albolineatus*.

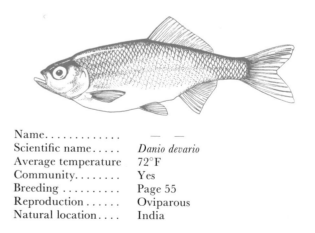

Name............	— —
Scientific name.....	*Danio devario*
Average temperature	72°F
Community........	Yes
Breeding..........	Page 55
Reproduction......	Oviparous
Natural location....	India

D. devario has a greenish body lightening to white on the belly. The forepart of the body is blue, and to the rear of this area are nine or so vertical yellowish stripes which diminish as they progress towards the tail. It is also prettily marked with three lateral blue lines with two yellow stripes in between them. The dorsal fin is white edged. The average length of adults is between 3½–4 in.

They are not difficult to spawn, and the procedure is the same as for the other danios.

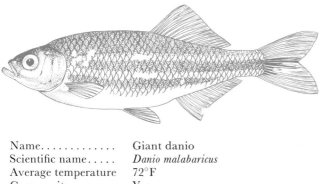

Name	Giant danio
Scientific name	*Danio malabaricus*
Average temperature	72°F
Community	Yes
Breeding	Page 55
Reproduction	Oviparous
Natural location	India

The giant danio is a fast, peaceful, ever-moving fish. It is the largest of the danios, and is an asset to any collection. It is related to the popular zebra fish (*Brachydanio rerio*), and its habits are similar.

The iridescent blue reflects a pale green as the fish swiftly changes direction. Front lighting shows its colours to their best advantage, but it is inconvenient to arrange.

It is well to remember when putting this fish into a community tank that it is likely to devour any very small fish, but this is, of course, liable to occur with any species if there is a large difference in size.

Sexing is difficult. The best method is to put six to a dozen in a tank (with other fish if accommodation is limited), and select the females when they become noticeably filled with spawn. They can then be separated and put into different tanks until required for breeding. Generally the golden yellow bars and vertical lines are more broken on the female than the male. The lower jaw of the female does not protrude as much as that of the male. But this method of sexing is not reliable. The giant danio is not generally easy to breed, as the eggs are adhesive and need plenty of plants in which to fall, but apart from this breeding follows the standard description. The number of eggs per spawning varies between 100 and 300, and they hatch within forty to sixty hours.

Name	Black shark
Scientific name	*Labeo chrysophekadion*
Average temperature	75°F
Community	Yes
Breeding	Not yet bred
Reproduction	Oviparous
Natural location	Siam, Dutch East Indies

One of the few really black tropicals, the black shark has a very attractive shark-like outline which is enhanced by the large dorsal fin which is invariably carried erect. As the fish ages, it has a tendency to lose its rich black colour and become a golden tint, starting at the caudal fin.

Aquarium specimens are quite hardy and can become quite large, 10-in. long, in fact, and in their natural environment grow up to 2 ft.

The black shark has a small, sucker-like mouth, and is virtually harmless to other fish. It likes to scavenge on the bottom among the rocks and crowns of the plants. Unfortunately it has not as yet been bred in captivity and, therefore, the breeding habits are unknown.

Name	Harlequin
Scientific name	*Rasbora heteromorpha*
Average temperature	73°F
Community	Yes
Breeding	See below
Reproduction	Oviparous
Natural location	Malay Peninsula and Sumatra

R. heteromorpha is just another example of nature's versatility in colour design. The silvery forepart of

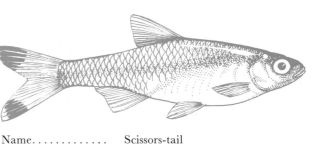

the body graduates into a rose pink as it nears the centre, which then carries right through to suffuse most of the tail. The dark marking, shown in the illustration above, from which it gets the popular name of harlequin, forms a triangle from the tail, ending in a curve over the spot where the pink and silver combine.

The sex can be determined in a fully developed fish by a golden line running along the top edge of the dark triangle. This is better coloured and more pronounced in the male. A further indication is the fuller belly of the female near breeding time.

Feeding on prepared foods keeps the harlequin in reasonable condition, but live foods should be given as often as possible to keep them in the best possible condition.

Breeding this species is extremely difficult; even the experts have not truly mastered the technique. The unknown quantity has yet to be found. The method as far as known is as follows. The temperature should be between 78° and 82°F, and old slightly acid water should be used in an aquarium containing broad-leafed plants such as *Sagittaria gigantea* or the larger *Cryptocorynes*. Courtship should commence within a day or two after the fish are introduced. The female will take up an inverted position, touching her belly on the underside of the leaves. Presently the male will join her, clasping her by curving his body around hers. During this embrace, one or two eggs are discharged on to the leaf, the female remaining in the inverted position.

The action is continued for about two hours and during this period somewhere between 30 and 80 eggs should be laid on the leaves of the plants. The eggs will hatch approximately 18 hours later provided that the water is kept at a temperature of 80°F.

Name..............	Scissors-tail
Scientific name.....	*Rasbora trilineata*
Average temperature	75°F
Community........	Yes
Breeding	See below
Reproduction	Oviparous
Natural location....	Malay Peninsula

Aquarium scissor-tails rarely exceed 3-in. long, although in the wild they have been found up to 8 in. They are peaceful, hardy, and make excellent community fish. The body is silver-white and somewhat translucent, with a dark line running along the middle of the side, and another line from just in front of the anal fin to the base of the lower lobe of the caudal fin. The distinctive tail is forked, often orange in colour, and tipped on each lobe with a black and white bar. When the fish is swimming the tail action is scissor-like, hence its popular name.

This species has been bred in captivity and it would seem that a water depth of about 5 in. is ideal, with a pH of 6·6–6·8. The temperature should be about 80°F and the tank should be large and well planted.

Several males should be used to a single female. Eggs will hatch in five to six days and the fry will grow rapidly on infusoria. When two weeks old, the fry can be given screened daphnia.

Helostoma rudolphi
Helostoma temmincki

106

Colisa lalia (opposite)
Trichogaster leeri (opposite)
Trichogaster trichopterus (opposite)
Aequidens portalegrensis
Aequidens latifrons
Cichlasoma biocellatum

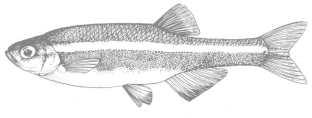

Name............ White Cloud Mountain minnow
Scientific name..... *Tanichthys albonubes*
Average temperature 68°F
Community........ Yes
Breeding.......... Page 55
Reproduction...... Oviparous
Natural location.... White Cloud Mountains, Nr. Canton

This sparkling little fish is fondly referred to as 'the poor man's neon tetra'. The coupling of its name with such an aristocrat is not surprising, for although it is not so startling in colour, it has the neon quality of iridescence.

Body colouring is generally between a silvery olive and violet-blue, with a fluorescent line of electric blue-green running from just behind the eye along the side of the body to the tail. Further enchantment is added by a red base to the dorsal fin and a streak through the tail.

The White Cloud Mountain minnow is quite a hardy species. It can stand a considerable temperature range of 40°–90°F, but do not try to keep them in such varying conditions. Peaceful, attractive, and easy to feed, they do prefer a little and often, instead of one big feed a day.

The average length for a fully grown specimen is 1¼ in., but unfortunately, as they increase in size, their brilliance diminishes. They are at their best when only ten to fourteen weeks old.

The dorsal fin can be used as an indication to sex; it is longer in the male.

The best breeding temperature is between 68° and 75°F. Courtship is much the same as with the danios—the male chases and the female scatters eggs freely.

The best method of preparing the aquarium for spawning is with a fine-leafed plant, such as *Myriophyllum*, loosely anchored with thin strips of lead to form a dense mat on the bottom of the tank. Water depth should be no more than 6 in. It is possible to spawn this species without any plants, although as a safety measure planting is probably most advisable.

Breeding traps for the White Clouds are the same as those for danios. In particular these traps can be used if your fish are likely to spawn when you will not be available to remove them immediately afterwards.

Cichlasoma severum
Cichlasoma meeki
Cichlasoma nigrofasciatum

Anabantids

The Anabantids belong to the order Perciformes, sub-order Anabantoidei and are grouped under the family Anabantidae.

The Anabantids are labyrinthic fish, that is they possess accessory organs, situated above the gills, for retaining air for breathing. They are all relatively small fish.

Name............ Climbing perch
Scientific name..... *Anabas testudineus*
Average temperature 76°F
Community........ No
Breeding.......... See below
Reproduction...... Oviparous
Natural location.... India, Malay Region, Burma, Siam, S. China, Ceylon and the Philippines

The body colour is a rich brown or olive, and the fins are usually a tint of brown. On some specimens the tail fin is a beautiful dark red.

Although these fish are labyrinthic fish, they do not conform to the usual breeding procedure of producing a bubble nest, instead the eggs are left free to float on the surface, where they hatch in one day at a temperature of 75°–80°F, that is if you are *very* fortunate. Successful breeding in an aquarium is practically unknown.

These fish are mainly nocturnal, and are invariably pugnacious, therefore they are not good citizens for the community tank. Food should consist mainly of animal foods, preferably fed in little pieces, but these fish will eat almost anything.

The climbing perch can survive long periods out of water providing its breathing organs are kept moist by occasional dips in water, or by humidity in the atmosphere.

When travelling overland, the fish supports itself by its strong pectoral fins and moves forward by extending the gill plates and rocking its body. The edges of the gill plates are serrated and this helps the fish to grip when climbing out of a pool.

Name............ Siamese fighter
Scientific name..... *Betta splendens*
Average temperature 73°F
Community........ No (yes, if only one)
Breeding.......... Page 56
Reproduction...... Oviparous
Natural location.... Siam

Siamese fighters are individualists—there is no other aquarium fish quite like them.

Almost every aquarist possesses at least one male, even if he has no intention of breeding. The extraordinary beauty of the Siamese fighter is sufficient to warrant it a place of honour in any community tank.

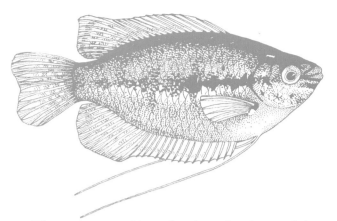

The male, when fully grown, develops a long flowing anal fin, a high dorsal fin, and a large flowing rounded tail. Another characteristic feature is the spear-shaped ventrals which are thrust forward in a menacing manner when the fish are angry.

You can only truly appreciate the beauty of this species when it is angry. A mirror placed on the side of the aquarium, so as to give the impression of another fish, causes an immediate fighting attitude, with gill plates ruffled and all the fins stiffly erect. This is a really wonderful sight.

'Cornflower blue' and 'fiery red' are the two main colours, but there are many colour variations in blue, green, and red, all with a metallic tint which is heightened when the fish is annoyed.

The fine fellow we know today has been developed from comparatively drab forefathers, which had smaller fins and a yellowish-brown body colouring with faint horizontal bands.

It is advisable to have only one male in a tank containing other fish, and if the tank is particularly large you may also add a female.

The fighters normally give the impression of good-natured indolence, preferring to lounge in a corner, or slowly cruise around the tank with eel-like movements.

You can identify sexes by the longer and more pointed finnage of the male. This does not become apparent until they are about an inch in length, and at this stage you should rear the males in separate containers, but females may be left together.

The fighters are very adaptable and soon settle down in new surroundings. They take readily to dry foods, but they fare better on daphnia and a live diet.

Breeding follows the standard method for bubble nesters, but it is rather an unreliable species because of its inborn aggressiveness. They breed at a temperature of 78°F.

Name	Thick lipped gourami
Scientific name	*Colisa labiosa*
Average temperature	73°F
Community	Yes
Breeding	Page 56
Reproduction	Oviparous
Natural location	Burma

Attaining a length of 3¼ in., the thick lip gourami is not so particularly thick lipped as the name would have us believe. It is the squat mouth which gives this impression.

It lacks the more distinctive markings and colourings of the other gouramis in this book, but makes up for this by its lack of timidity.

Anabus testudineus

The sex can be determined by the shape of the dorsal fin which ends in a point on the male, and is slightly shorter and more rounded in the female.

It breeds according to the standard description at a temperature of 80°F. The eggs, which are transparent, float to the surface.

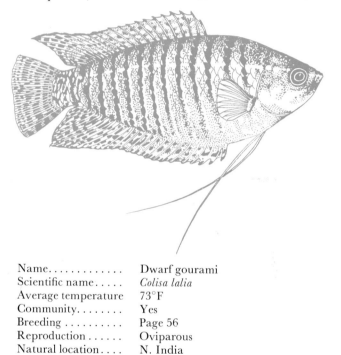

Name	Dwarf gourami
Scientific name	*Colisa lalia*
Average temperature	73°F
Community	Yes
Breeding	Page 56
Reproduction	Oviparous
Natural location	N. India

C. lalia is the smallest of the genus, but what it lacks in size it makes up for in beauty. The male, as may be expected, is the better coloured. The colour pattern of red and blue-green bands runs vertically across the body and tail, and scintillates during breeding.

Sex can be decided, in addition to the better colouring, by the pointed end to the dorsal fin of the male. A further check can be taken from the orange-red, feeler-like ventral fins.

Reasonably hardy, and normally peaceful to the point of timidity, the male dwarf gourami sometimes kills his mate during courtship.

Breeding follows the standard description for bubble nesters, except that pieces of fine plant leaves are woven into the nest. The breeding temperature is 80°F.

Name............	Kissing gourami
Scientific name.....	*Helostoma temmincki*
Average temperature	77°F
Community........	A single specimen only
Breeding	See below
Reproduction	Oviparous
Natural location....	Siam, Java, Borneo, Sumatra, and Malay Peninsular

It is a common human trait to credit animals, in this instance fish, with human reactions when their actions are similar to human behaviour. Therefore, when we find two fish lip to lip, they are assumed to be kissing, hence the popular name for *H. temmincki*.

It is true that this species will be seen sometimes 'kissing' but it does not mean that love is the motivation. It is, in fact, not part of the mating procedure, and the true reason for this behaviour is not known. However, it is an interesting exhibition.

The general body colour is a light greenish blue, lightening to silver on the belly. The sides are marked with thin, horizontal, wavy stripes and a dark bar crosses the tail root.

The spiny dorsal has a dark lateral strip running through the centre, and the spiny anal fin has a similar marking along its edge. The lips are thick and protruding, and are equipped with fine teeth—an arrangement ideally suited for eating algæ off rocks and plants.

H. temmincki is mainly a herbivorous species, as may be expected, and will eat dried foods, but it should also be fed with dried spinach and powdered oatmeal, and plenty of algæ should be provided.

It is not a ready breeder and does not build the usual bubble nest. After the usual chasing, the pair embrace and the female scatters between 20 and 50 eggs which float on the surface. This is repeated until between 350 and 2,000 eggs have been laid. As it is more than likely that these will be eaten between each embrace, it is advisable to remove the eggs promptly and transfer them to a container floating in the same aquarium. Once the spawning is completed, the adults can be removed and the eggs returned to their original home.

For breeding the temperature should be about 84°F and the water preferably at least 12-in. deep. The pH should be about 7·4—7·6. Eggs hatch in about three days.

Once the eggs hatch the problem of feeding the young fry presents itself. Little is known about the correct foods so this stage will prove to be largely experimental.

The average length of adults is about 5 in., but they grow to twice this size in the wild.

Betta splendens

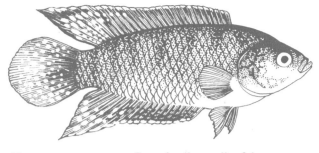

Name............	Round-tail paradise fish
Scientific name.....	*Macropodus chinensis*
Average temperature	70°F
Community........	Yes (but untrustworthy)
Breeding	Page 56
Reproduction	Oviparous
Natural location....	E. China and Korea

This species is very similar to *M. opercularis*. The most obvious difference is in the tail, which is rounded in both sexes. The body has slightly less red, and the markings are less distinctive. The male may be identified by his more vivid colouring and larger fins.

At breeding time the body of the male becomes suffused with blue-black, and speckled with numerous light coloured spots.

Adults attain a length of 3 in.

These are peaceful fish and they are not worried by lower temperatures—65°–73°F being an average range. Keep temperature always below the 75°F mark.

Name............	Paradise fish
Scientific name.....	*Macropodus opercularis*
Average temperature	70°F
Community........	Yes (but untrustworthy)
Breeding	Page 56
Reproduction	Oviparous
Natural location....	China

Because of its pugnaciousness, the paradise fish is generally shunned by aquarists who have limited accommodation. This is rather a pity for it is a beautiful and interesting species. It will eat any foods, but has a preference for daphnia and a live diet. Extremely hardy, the paradise fish can stand a temperature range of 50°–90°F, and is easily tamed. This may at first sound ridiculous for a fish, but nevertheless it is not long before it will accept tit-bits from the fingers of its owner.

The body colouring is a deep rusty red with emerald stripes. The long pointed filaments of the caudal fin, which are present on the male only, are usually emerald and end in a very pale blue. The females have a more rounded tail and shorter fin tips.

Normally there is little to choose between the colouring of the sexes, but as spawning time approaches the male becomes more vivid, whilst the female becomes paler and paler, until she is

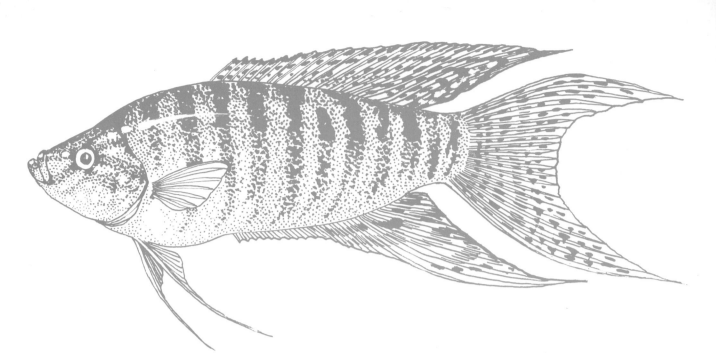

finally a drab white.

Adult paradise fish grow to about 3 in., and whilst they can be put into a community tank it is advisable not to have the other occupants too small in comparison.

Paradise fish are common in the rice fields of China, where they have a plentiful supply of food in the form of mosquito larvæ.

They breed in the standard method for bubble nesters, at a temperature of 75°F.

Although classed as tropical, these fish can stand temperatures down to about 50°F. During the summer months they could, therefore, be cultured in a pond.

Name.............	Lace or pearl gourami
Scientific name.....	*Trichogaster leeri*
Average temperature	73°F
Community........	Yes
Breeding..........	Page 56
Reproduction......	Oviparous
Natural location....	Siam, Malay Peninsular, Sumatra

One of the comparatively larger aquarium fish, the pearl gourami grows to about 4 in. It is the most attractive of the gouramis, with a body colouring of turquoise suffused with mosaic pearly dots, not unlike exquisitely fine lace. A jagged, dark brown line runs from the mouth through the eye, and fades away as it approaches the tail. The ventral fins are long and slender, and are often carried pointing forward.

The pearl gouramis are timid and they tend to hide behind plants and rocks. This is their only drawback.

During the breeding period, the throat and breast of the male will turn a rich golden rust colour.

They make exceedingly good parents, as neither the female nor the male is very inclined to eat the eggs or young and rarely, if ever, do the males attack the females during courtship; this is unusual for this type of breeder. Breeding follows the standard description and the temperature should be approximately 80°F. The number of eggs that are laid is usually quite considerable.

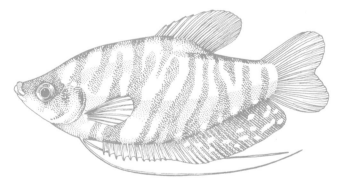

Name.............	Snakeskin gourami
Scientific name.....	*Trichogaster pectoralis*
Average temperature	75°F
Community........	Yes
Breeding..........	Page 56
Reproduction......	Oviparous
Natural location....	Indo-China to Malaysia

Aquarists may be surprised to learn that the snakeskin gourami grows to about 12-in. long in its home waters, and provides a popular fish dish in Ceylon. However, aquarium specimens rarely grow longer than 6 in.

The body colour is a greenish brown, overlaid with pale yellow-gold wavy bars. It is marked with a dark brown to black broken line along the sides.

Helostoma temmincki
Trichogaster leeri

116

The fins are varying tints of yellow. The iris of the eye is outstandingly yellow. Sexes can be recognised by the much higher dorsal fin of the male.

These fish are hardy and very good natured, and are among the easier bubble nesters to breed. Spawnings are usually large, and neither the eggs nor the fry are eaten by the parents. They breed at a temperature of 78°–82°F.

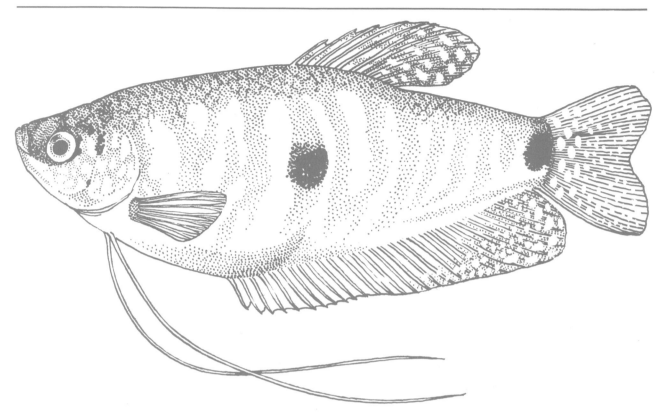

Name	Three spot gourami
Scientific name	*Trichogaster trichopterus*
Average temperature	73°F
Community	Yes
Breeding	Page 56
Reproduction	Oviparous
Natural location	India, Malay Peninsula, Indo-China

Easily the most common of the gouramis, the three spot gourami is an unbelievable powder blue in colour, overlaid with a wavy pattern like a water mark. Two black dots on the body, one about centre, the other near the tail, together with the eye, form the three spots from which it gets the popular name. The ventral fins are long and hair-like, and are usually stretched forward as if used as feelers.

The three spot is 5-in. long when fully grown, and tends to bully smaller fish.

Sexing is by the dorsal fin, as for other gouramis, and breeding follows the standard description.

Cichlids

The Cichlids belong to the order Perciformes (which includes the Percomorphi), sub-order Percoidei, and are grouped under the family Cichlidae. They are perch-like, spiny-rayed fish, and have only one nostril on each side of the nose.

In general they include the larger aquarium species, and the most pugnacious, although there are a few exceptions. The Cichlids are not usually good citizens for the community tank. They are much better suited to large aquaria, and then only in single pairs.

During breeding they have a habit of up-rooting plants, possibly in search of enemies.

Name	Blue Acara
Scientific name	*Aequidens latifrons*
Average temperature	76°F
Community	No
Breeding	Page 57
Reproduction	Oviparous
Natural location	Panama and Colombia

One of the best known Cichlids, the blue acara is a prolific breeder and of peaceful disposition. A fully grown blue acara will average 6-in. long and so plenty of space should be allowed.

The body colouring is mainly of a greenish hue, with darker bands running vertically along the body. Under the eye, and in the centre of the body, are two dark spots. Irregular lines on the head, mostly in a horizontal direction, are blue with a

Aequidens portalegrensis

118

phosphorescent quality. Scales on the upper part of the body are blue with brownish edges, and the lower half is the reverse. The fins are mostly dull orange with a sprinkling of blue-green markings. Both sexes are coloured alike, but the males have the typical long filament to the dorsal fin.

The temperature of the water should be 70°–85°F, and blue acaras can be bred in the normal manner at a temperature of 78°F.

Name	Brown Acara
Scientific name	*Aequidens portalegrensis*
Average temperature	75°F
Community	No
Breeding	Page 57
Reproduction	Oviparous
Natural location	S.E. Brazil

This fish is one of the kindlier Cichlids. It grows to a length of 5–6 in., and is similar to the blue acara in colouring, but is far more subdued. It is quite easy to breed, even in smallish aquaria.

Sexing is not easy. An indication of the male is that he has more spangles, which are most noticeable on the tail.

Another distinctive feature of this species is the large, blunt head.

Name	Jack Dempsey
Scientific name	*Cichlasoma biocellatum*
Average temperature	75°F
Community	No
Breeding	Page 57
Reproduction	Oviparous
Natural location	South America

The Jack Dempsey is an old aquarium favourite, and it is not surprising when one contemplates the beautiful colouring. Mature fish have a body colour of a deep blue-green with blue spots. The dorsal fin is edged with red.

As the fish matures the colours become less volatile and brilliant.

It is a hardy species, growing to 7-in. long, and it is an excellent breeder and parent.

Cichlasoma biocellatum

Name	Chocolate cichlid
Scientific name	*Cichlasoma coryphaenoides*
Average temperature	75°F
Community	No (see below)
Breeding	Page 57
Reproduction	Oviparous
Natural location	Brazil. Argentina

Although a considerable number of fish vary their colour depending upon mood and emotion, the chocolate cichlid is noted, not only for its range of colour changing, but also for the speed in which it achieves the change. Under normal conditions the general body colour is pale to dark brown and the belly is a beautiful, metallic purple-brown.

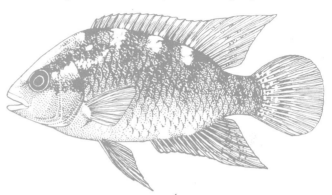

The sides are marked by dark vertical bands. It is also marked with three dark smudges, one on the gill cover, a second on the centre of the body, and a third on the tail root. The fins are generally brownish, and the dorsal fin has a red edge.

These are quite large fish, 6–7 in. being about average length for the adults, and they can be trouble makers. To the best knowledge of the author they have not been bred in aquaria. They are aggressive fish during mating, and it is not unusual for one fish to actually kill its partner.

Name	Chanchito
Scientific name	*Cichlasoma facetum*
Average temperature	75°F
Community	Only small specimens
Breeding	Page 57
Reproduction	Oviparous
Natural location	Argentina

It is the size only of the chanchito that excludes it from the community tank. Adults attain a length of 7-in. and, except at breeding time, they are not aggressive. Small specimens up to about 3 in. may be included in the community tank.

The body colour is pale brown overlaid with six or seven dark vertical bars. Some specimens also have a dark line running down the lateral line. The iris of the eye is red. The chanchito has much to commend it as an introductory species of the Cichlids. It is easy to breed in the standard manner, and the adults make excellent parents. Their feeding habits are typical of the Cichlids.

Name............	Firemouth
Scientific name.....	*Cichlasoma meeki*
Average temperature	75°F
Community........	No
Breeding..........	Page 57
Reproduction......	Oviparous
Natural location....	Yucatan

Some tropical fish are so startling in their beauty that they set themselves apart from all others. The firemouth is one of these because its colouring is surely unique. The green-blue body is shaded irregularly with a pale purple, and has an irregular, broken, dark line running from just behind the gill plate to the tail. The first outstanding feature is the fiery red or deep orange belly. This colour runs from the tail base, along the belly, and *right into the mouth*, forming a triangle just behind the gill plate. The second notable feature of the firemouth is the bright green-edged spot on the base of the gill plate. Various shades of red are found on the fins.

Up to 3-in. long, the sexes are indistinguishable, but as they grow larger, the male develops the usual elongated point to the rear of the dorsal. Fully grown fish will reach a length of 4–5 in. Small specimens may be kept in a community tank, but it is advisable to keep large fish in a tank on their own. The tank should be spacious.

The firemouth breeds in the standard manner at a temperature of 80°F, when the colouring tends to become more intense, especially in the female.

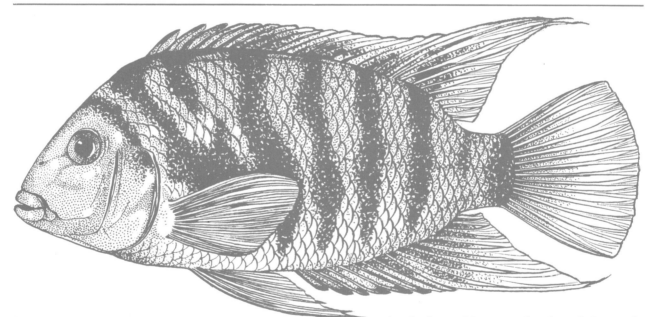

Name............	Zebra cichlid
Scientific name.....	*Cichlasoma nigrofasciatum*
Average temperature	75°F
Community........	No
Breeding..........	Page 57
Reproduction......	Oviparous
Natural location....	Central America

The zebra cichlid is a highly strung nervous fish, which dashes about the aquarium from one refuge to another, at a very fast speed. It is also fond of lying under an archway of piled stones.

Like most nervous fish, the colouring and markings of the zebra are volatile—very pronounced one minute and almost gone the next. The body colouring varies from yellowish-white to light grey, the darker stripes on the sides extend into the dorsal fin, and there are yellowish spots between the dark markings on the dorsal. Emerald green outlines the sawtooth edges of the dorsal and anal fins.

Strangely enough, the zebra is a fish where the female boasts the better markings. Although the male has the same colouring, the female has more brilliance.

Extremely warlike, it is essential to keep specimens over 2-in. long in a tank on their own. Even at this size they will attack more peaceful fish. Their method of attack is to charge the victim with their hard heads, which soon kills. The jaws are so strong that they can crush a snail shell with one vicious snap. Fully grown adults reach 4 in.

It breeds according to the standard description at a temperature of 80°F, but you should add plenty of rocks and stone arches to provide protection for the weaker partner. This is not always the female, but the smaller of the two.

The depressions in the sand in which the babies are reared are nearly always hidden from view behind a rock or stone. A family is indicated if the parents seem interested in some shady nook.

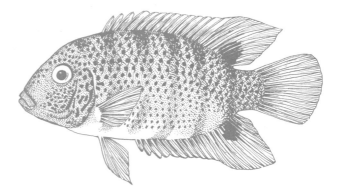

Name.............	Striped cichlid
Scientific name.....	*Cichlasoma severum*
Average temperature	75°F
Community........	No (unless very small)
Breeding..........	Page 57
Reproduction......	Oviparous
Natural location....	Guiana and Amazon Basin

Body coloration is generally blue-green, dark green, yellow-brown, brown or nearly black, and whatever the basic colour may be it can vary considerably with the temper or mood of the fish. A dark vertical stripe marks the rear of the body from the dorsal fin down into the base of the anal fin. A paler dark bar crosses the tail root. The head and gill covers are lightly marked with irregular dark markings, and the body of the male is covered by lateral rows of reddish dots, darker on the upper body. The fins are red-brown or orange.

Aquarium specimens will grow to about 7 in. They are hardy, and not so aggressive as most of the large members of the family. They are not easily bred, but breed according to the standard description. As only the males have the rows of reddish dots, sexing will not prove any problem.

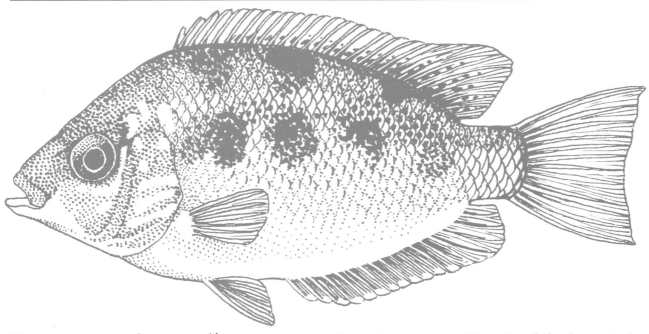

Name.............	Orange chromide
Scientific name.....	*Etroplus maculatus*
Average temperature	78°F
Community........	Yes (usually)
Breeding..........	Page 57
Reproduction......	Oviparous
Natural location....	India and Ceylon

The orange chromide is one of the few Cichlids that can usually be included in a community tank. It grows to about 3-in. long and has an orange-gold body, darkening to olive along the back, and sprinkled with orderly rows of small red dots. Three large bluish spots are arranged along the lateral line. Immediately below the eye it has a light blue crescent. The dorsal fin is sandy in colour, and the pelvic and anal fins are similar but darker in hue.

It is a fish that likes warmth; ideally it prefers a temperature between 75° and 82°F. It is not an easy species to spawn; the dark coloured eggs are suspended by individual threads from the leaves of plants. Alternatively, if a flower pot is put in the aquarium, the eggs may be suspended from the inside top edge. Otherwise spawning is as detailed for Cichlids.

The eggs hatch in about five days, and the fry tend to have a preference for following mother. Adults should be removed after about two weeks.

Name	Egyptian mouthbreeder
Scientific name	*Haplochromis multicolor*
Average temperature	75° F
Community	Yes (if care is taken)
Breeding	Page 57 and below
Reproduction	Oviparous
Natural location	Egypt

This fish, from the land of the Pharaohs, is an example of the lengths to which nature will go to protect the young of certain species.

The ground colour of the body is generally metallic green. Other colours from blue to orange are found on the body and fins, varying with different specimens. The tints in the fins often include black and yellow, and are more varied in the male. A sex indication is the red tip on the anal fin, which usually identifies the male. Like most fish, the Egyptian mouthbreeders are seen at their best when in breeding condition. At other times they are a yellowish-grey.

Fully grown specimens only reach a length of 2½ in. and can be included in the community tank, but you should take care as they are quite likely to attack and kill smaller fish.

The breeding tank should be planted with plenty of oxygenating plants, leaving plenty of space between the plants. The male fans a depression in the sand into which the female lays her eggs, and these are fertilised as they fall down into the depression. The ideal breeding temperature is 77°F. Any number between 20 and 200 may be dropped in one spawning, and then, contrary to the usual habits of the Cichlids, the female picks them up and carries them around in her mouth. (She actually holds them in the buccal cavity.) The eggs are not only ca   ed until they hatch, but until the fry absorb their yolk-sac, which they do in a matter of 14 to 15 days. During this period the female stolidly refuses to eat. This seems to be nature's precaution against the eggs being swallowed.

Even after the young have reached the stage of free swimming, they are liable to dart back into the protection of the female's mouth, if they are small enough, at the first sign of danger.

Whilst the eggs are incubating, and even after they are hatched, all mouthbreeders work their mouth in a peculiar chewing motion, which ensures a good circulation of water around the eggs.

The self-imposed task of the female takes its toll of her vitality, and after two weeks she looks a strange fish with a large head and emaciated body. Owing to the strain breeding puts upon her, it is not advisable to spawn too frequently. Three times a year should be considered a maximum.

Remove the male after spawning. This is best done in semi-darkness, using a dark coloured net so as not to frighten or cause the female to swallow her eggs. The female should be removed when the fry are strong enough, which is usually after 25 days. The fry should be fed with infusoria after 14 to 15 days, when the fry first leave the mouth.

Name	Jewel cichlid
Scientific name	*Hemichromis bimaculatus*
Average temperature	75° F
Community	No
Breeding	Page 57 and below
Reproduction	Oviparous
Natural location	Tropical Africa

Under normal conditions the body colour is an olive green, darker on the back, and a lighter

Hemichromis bimaculatus

orange yellow on the belly. The body is marked with a few blurred vertical dark bars, a dark spot just below the dorsal fin at about the centre of the body, and a spot on the tail root. Another spot is situated on the gill cover, and a dark line passes through the eye.

It is only at breeding times that the full beauty of these fish can be appreciated. The lower part of the body then becomes a rich red, and the upper part becomes a dark olive which reflects a red sheen. Metallic blue spots are present on the head, body and fins, and the major fins have red edgings.

Sexes are similar, but it will be found that the male has larger metallic spots on the gill covers, and a crescent pattern of spots on the tail. Adults attain a length of about 4 in.

The jewel cichlids are definitely 'bad actors' and should have an aquarium to themselves. Breeding is similar to the standard description at a temperature of 80°F, but they are difficult fish to pair, and it is possible that the female may be attacked and even killed during an attempted, or even successful, mating.

It is a good plan to have plenty of rocks and large-leafed plants in the breeding tank to provide a safe refuge for the young fish. After about six weeks the young fish are likely to attack each other, so it is obvious why a tank no smaller than 24 in. × 12 in. × 12 in. should be used.

Providing very clean conditions exist, it is possible to raise the fry from ova without the assistance of their parents.

Name.............	Angel fish
Scientific name.....	*Pterophyllum eimekei*
Average temperature	75°F
Community........	Yes
Breeding..........	See below
Reproduction......	Oviparous
Natural location....	Amazon and Guiana

The long backward flowing fins of the angel fish give the fish the appearance of a butterfly or bird with outspread wings, as it gracefully swims among the plants.

The silver body, overcast with blue, has many specks, not unlike small freckles, on the sides. Evenly spaced black bars stripe the body, the first passing through the eye, which is red, and the last is on the tail. The ventral fins of the angel are long and thin, and curve back gracefully under the fish. The dark bars, which is nature's camouflage, practically disappear when they are frightened.

Unlike most Cichlids they are good community fish, and they do not worry the plants. They will, of course, make a meal of any very small fish if given the chance.

Sometimes angel fish lose their appetite for no apparent reason. It is advisable when this hap-

pens to try a change of diet. Try such foods as daphnia, chopped earthworm, white worm, and mosquito larvæ. If this fails, a change of water may induce them to eat.

Sexing is most difficult. There are several methods, but most of them are unreliable. Probably the best indication is the appearance of the breeding tube just before spawning. This is more pointed in the male and is carried at a more forward angle. Experts can tell by the shape of the body, but it is extremely difficult for the layman to do so. It may be judged by the forward part of the body between the long ventrals and the beginning of the anal fins. In the female, however, this outline appears longer and straighter than in the male of the species.

Breeding habits are a little different from the standard description. The young are not placed on stones or in depressions in the sand, but remain stuck to the plants on which they were hatched. Plenty of broad-leafed plants, such as *Vallisneria* or *Sagittaria* should be put into the breeding tank for the eggs, which are adhesive and are laid on these strong plants.

A bamboo cane or glass tube, the inside of which has been coloured to make it opaque, stuck into the sand just slightly off the vertical may also be used as an artificial spawning ground. Most professional breeders use this method, as the eggs are then easily removed to another tank for rearing the fry.

It is a problem as to whether the parents should be removed immediately after a spawning, although it is certainly safer. While it is a pretty sight to see parents and young together, there is a fifty-fifty chance of them being eaten.

During the period when the young are attached to the leaf, they are continually picked up in the mouth of their parents, held for a few moments, and then sprayed on to another leaf. The reason for this seems to be cleanliness. If you transplant the young to another tank at this stage, mild aeration helps to produce conditions of strict cleanliness.

After hatching, the fry usually become free swimmers in about two days, when micro-worm and sifted daphnia should be given.

Angel fish prefer slightly acid water.

Silversides

The silversides also belong to the super-order Atherinomorpha, sub-order Atherinoidei and are grouped under the family Atherinidae. The

Melanotaenia nigrans
Etroplus maculatus
Pterophyllum eimekei

majority of the species is found in coastal waters, but a few have taken to fresh water. The double or split dorsal, i.e. first spiny, second soft, is a major characteristic.

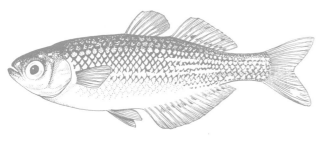

Name.	Australian rainbow
Scientific name.	*Melanotænia nigrans*
Average temperature	70°F
Community.	Yes
Breeding	Page 55
Reproduction	Oviparous
Natural location. . . .	Australia

The silversides are common saltwater fish, found in nearly all temperate waters. The Australian rainbow is one of the few that inhabit fresh water permanently.

Strangely enough, few of our present-day aquarium fish come from Australia, but this peaceful beauty is an exception.

The body of the Australian rainbow is mainly silver, faintly overcast with a warmish pink which runs into the centre of the tail. The scales are edged with dark brown and each one is clearly discernible as if it were carefully drawn. The base of the scale has a thicker line, which forms distinct horizontal bars along the sides. In daylight the scales have a spectrum-coloured sheen, which is the reason for the name rainbow.

The eye, with its dark centre, has a phosphorescent outer-circle, which reflects any stray beam of light. The dark spot on the gill cover also has a luminous quality.

These fish are ideal aquarium members. They are easily fed and hardy, and can stand a temperature range of between 60° and 90°F.

Sexing is not easy, although the male is smaller and slimmer with more brilliant colouring. They may be bred quite successfully in the aquarium in the same way as the egg-layers.

Nandids

The Nandids belong to the order Perciformes, sub-order Percoidei and are grouped under the

Scatophagus argus
Badis badis
Corydoras aeneus

family Nandidae. The Nandids differ from their related families mainly in skeleton structure. Generally they possess large mouths, capable of opening out to a relatively great extent, almost transparent caudal fins, and clear parts in the rear of their anal and dorsal fins.

The family is small, and related only to India, Siam, Burma and the Malay Peninsula.

Name.	— —
Scientific name.	*Badis badis*
Average temperature	75°F
Community.	Yes
Breeding	See below
Reproduction	Oviparous
Natural location. . . .	India

The Nandids differ from their related families mainly in skeleton formation. Generally they have large mouths capable of opening out to a relatively great extent. The majority of Nandids also have almost transparent caudal fins, and clear parts in the rear of their anal and dorsal fins. Nandids are widely distributed.

Strangely, the *Badis badis* is a Nandid that has neither the transparent finnage nor the elastic mouth: it is nevertheless an interesting fish. Fully grown specimens attain a length of 2–3 in. The male is usually longer, but this is not a reliable indication of sex, neither is the colouring. However, the males do tend to become more intense and darker when in breeding condition, whilst the females remain normal. It is rather difficult to describe the colouring of these fish as it varies so much with temperament. It can vary between a light red to a dark scarlet, blue and deep mauve. A dark bar runs through the eye. The causes of colour variation are many—the presence of other fish, fright, and water conditions for example.

Another characteristic of *Badis badis* is the hollow underparts which give the impression of wasting. It also adopts unusual positions in the water and when it is immobile it does not seem to mind its body being at any angle.

The *Badis badis* is rather a peaceful fish and is actually shy despite its rather pugnacious appearance. It prefers to hide away among the plants

during the day and really becomes active at dusk.

Adult females are fuller bodied than the male. which retains the hollow underparts. These fish prefer live foods which should be generally supplied; dried foods other than in small quantities are not advisable

For breeding, the temperature should be raised to 80°F, and a clean flower pot laid horizontally on the floor of the aquarium. The eggs are laid on the inside of the upper surface. The female should be removed immediately after spawning. The male will then tend the eggs by fanning them until the young hatch, which is between 60 and 72 hours. When the young become free swimmers, the male should also be removed.

Loaches

Loaches belong to the super-order Ostariophysi, sub-order Cyprinoidei, and are grouped under the family Cobitidae. They have much in common with the carps, but differ in having three or more pairs of barbels, and they never have teeth in the jaw.

Loaches can survive in damp mud, and damp pockets of dried up pools, by using their intestines for the respiratory function instead of their gills. They are exclusively all Old World species.

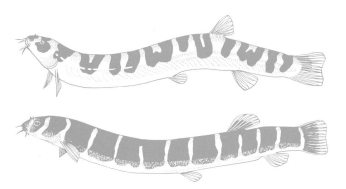

Name	Malayan loach
Scientific name	*Acanthophthalmus semicinctus*
Average temperature	75°F
Community	Yes
Breeding	—
Reproduction	Oviparous
Natural location	Malay Peninsula and Archipelago

The Malayan loach, also known as snake fish, snake worm, half banded coolie, and Malayan eel, at a quick glance could easily be mistaken for a tiny eel. Although decidedly eel-like, a second glance soon corrects the first impression.

The main body colouring is of a salmon pink hue, but this colour will vary with different specimens from pink to beige or orange with a distinct

Pterophyllum eimekei

pinkish colouring near the gills. The dark markings are brown and form half bands; these bands are on the upper part of the body and are not regular in shape. They may even have a light spot. Two of the maxillary barbels are on the tip of the snout. Specimens offered for sale in this country rarely exceed 2 in.

A. semicinctus has sometimes in the past become confused with a similar species—*A. kuhlii. A. kuhlii* can be identified by comparison of the dark markings which extend from the back right down to the underparts.

Other species in the genus are *A. kuhlii kuhlii*, a sub-species from Java, and *A. kuhlii sumatranus*, another sub-species from Sumatra which has less bands and wider interspaces. Borneo's contribution is *A. shelfordi* with dark bands tapering as they near the lower portion of the body. A second row of patchy markings are placed between the main markings.

The Malayan loach is a scavenger, and is quite useful in clearing up any food left uneaten by other fish. It is a nocturnal fish, lying up most of the day behind rocks, or hidden in among the plants. It will, however, soon learn to become active during the day, once acclimatised.

Little is known about their breeding habits at present

Catfish

The catfish belong to the super-order Ostariophysi, order Siluriformes, and are grouped under 31 families. The principal families covered in this section are as follows:

Callichthyidae	Small armoured catfish.
Siluridae	Catfish with very long anal fins and small, or absent, dorsal fins.
Doradidae	Heavy bodied with a single row of bony plates, each of which bear a spine, running along the centre of each side of the fish.
Bagridae	Unarmoured catfish with long barbels. Old World.
Pimelodidae	Unarmoured catfish with long barbels. New World.
Bunocephalidae	Unarmoured catfish with flat heads.
Loricariidae	Spiny armoured catfish with sucking disc mouths.

Catfish never have scales, but some species are partly or completely covered with bony plates, and the vast majority have barbels.

Name............	Bronze catfish
Scientific name.....	*Corydoras aeneus*
Average temperature	70°F
Community........	Yes
Breeding	See *Corydoras paleatus*
Reproduction	Oviparous
Natural location....	South America

This fish grows to about 2¾ in., and is an excellent scavenger. The head is quite rounded, the body is thick set, and the whiskers are small. The body colouring is a beautiful shaded bronze-green without any pattern markings.

The bronze catfish is found naturally in Trinidad.

Name............	— —
Scientific name.....	*Corydoras agassizi*
Average temperature	70°F
Community........	Yes
Breeding	—
Reproduction	Oviparous
Natural location....	Amazon

This is one of the slightly larger aquarium catfish, and will attain a length of about 3½ in. It has the typical appearance of a catfish, with a particularly flat underside and spade-like head. The forepart of the dorsal fin is dark grey, and the tail rather prettily flecked with orderly rows of spots.

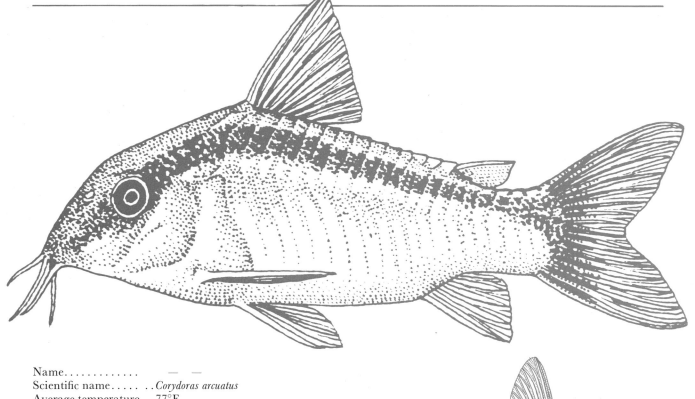

Name............	— —
Scientific name......	. . *Corydoras arcuatus*
Average temperature	77°F
Community........	Yes
Breeding	—
Reproduction	Oviparous
Natural location....	Upper Amazon

The body colour of this fish is silvery white with a greenish-blue overall sheen. It is marked with a dark curving line from the eye, along the upper part of the body, to the base of the caudal fin. The male fish often has this line starting a little distance behind the eye.

Adult fish attain a length of 2½ in., but to the author's knowledge they have not yet been bred in captivity.

This fish is very typical of the Corydoras family and is obviously much happier when it is a member of a small group.

Corydoras arcuatus is usually a lively fellow and an interesting species to observe.

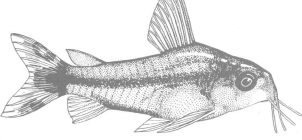

Name............	Dwarf catfish
Scientific name.....	*Corydoras hastatus*
Average temperature	78°F
Community........	Yes
Breeding	See below
Reproduction	Oviparous
Natural location....	Amazon Basin

This tiny little catfish only grows to about 1¾ in. and is quite an attractive little fellow with a grey-

Corydoras aenus

Corydoras agassizi

green body, marked with a dark stripe starting from just behind the pectoral fins and terminating in a large spot on the tail base. The spot is outlined with a horse-shoe of white.

This species is not too difficult to breed. The eggs are deposited individually on the sides of the aquarium, on stones, and on the leaves of plants.

Name..............	Leopard catfish
Scientific name.....	*Corydoras julii*
Average temperature	70°F
Community........	Yes
Breeding..........	—
Reproduction......	Oviparous
Natural location....	East and North East Brazil

The leopard catfish is quite a popular fish. Its body colouring is a whitish-grey, peppered with black spots. These spots extend over the nose, and also form roughly three lateral lines along the body. The dorsal fin has a black spot on its upper half, and the tail fin also carries a series of almost symmetrical spots. Fully grown specimens are not very large—about $2\frac{1}{2}$-in. long.

Whilst it is generally accepted that catfish are scavengers and rely mostly on left-overs, the aquarist would be well advised to consider their diet seriously if he would like to *attempt* to breed them. They are, however, seldom bred.

Name..............	Blue catfish
Scientific name.....	*Corydoras nattereri*
Average temperature	70°F
Community........	Yes
Breeding..........	See below
Reproduction......	Oviparous
Natural location....	Central and North Brazil

The blue catfish has a silvery brown body with a translucent overtone of blue. It is marked with a dark stripe from caudal fin to gill cover. The fins are usually clear and unpatterned, but occasionally the dorsal fin may have a dark tip. The eyes are golden. Aquarium specimens can be expected to attain a length of about $2\frac{1}{2}$ in.

This is not an easy fish to breed but if you wish to try, use the method described for *C. paleatus*.

Name..............	— —
Scientific name.....	*Corydoras paleatus*
Average temperature	72°F
Community........	Yes
Breeding..........	See below
Reproduction......	Oviparous
Natural location....	Argentina and South East Brazil

This catfish is probably the most common of the catfish. It is not unattractive, the main body colour is a yellowish hue shot with a few green scales here

Corydoras julii

Corydoras nattereri

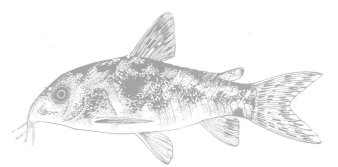

and there. These are more pronounced about the head. The dark overmarkings are irregular and coloured blue-black. The pectoral fins are yellow, the anal and ventral fins are opaque ivory, and the tail and dorsal fins are almost clear, but marked with dark flecks. Fully grown aquarium specimens attain a length of $2\frac{3}{4}$ in.

C. paleatus can be bred, but may prove inconsistent. To have any success at all, the first consideration must be the condition of the fish. Generally, the catfish are regarded as scavengers, and quite rightly, but fish intended for breeding should not be considered so. Separate them and feed in the usual manner for breeding. Daphnia, tubifex etc. are the best foods for this purpose. In fact, plenty of live foods should be provided.

The breeding tank should be an established one and thickly planted at one end with *Sagittaria*. The tank should have a capacity of 8–10 gallons and have a fair layer of 'mulm' on the bottom.

Sexing is not easy, but the most reliable sign is that the female is more round and full bodied.

As the female approaches a condition conducive to breeding, her belly takes on a reddish hue and the first ray of the pectoral fin also reddens. The first indication that spawning is likely to occur is when the male repeatedly swims over the back of the female, just touching her with his barbels.

Later the pair appear to embrace, the male almost on his back, the female in a right-angle position. They remain in this position for possibly 30 seconds, then break away to swim quite independently. The female, upon close inspection, can now be seen to carry about four eggs between her ventral fins. She next looks for a suitable spot to deposit them, carefully going over the plants with her mouth. She then clasps a leaf with her ventral fin and presses the eggs on it so that they adhere.

This action is repeated probably over a period of two hours, resulting in up to a hundred eggs being deposited. Remove the parents.

The eggs hatch in about four days and the young disappear into the sediment for about two weeks. During this period it is unnecessary to provide food. They will feed on the 'mulm'. If it is impossible to provide the necessary 'mulm', provide a little paste made from boiled oatmeal.

The breeding temperature is approximately 70°F and the water slightly alkaline (pH 7·2).

135

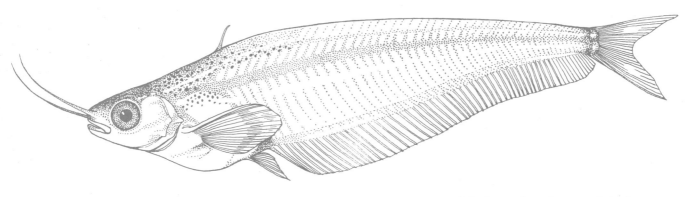

Name	Glass catfish
Scientific name	*Kryptopterus bicirrhus*
Average temperature	75°F
Community	Yes
Breeding	—
Reproduction	Oviparous
Natural location	Siam, Dutch East Indies

The glass catfish is an oddity from Malaya.

The body is *really* transparent. The skeleton is quite easily seen. If it were not for the silvery sac containing the internal organs, it would be difficult indeed to find the fish in any aquarium.

Another interesting feature is the long anal fin which occupies most of the ventral surface of the body. This fin has a wavy action not unlike a thin reed in quickly flowing water. The two barbels, which are comparatively long, hang from the upper lip. Fully grown specimens in the aquarium rarely exceed 2–3 in.

Glass catfish should be fed mainly with live food, but they will eat a small quantity of dried food. They are quite happy in a community tank at a temperature of 72°–82°F once they have become acclimatised.

Their breeding habits are unknown.

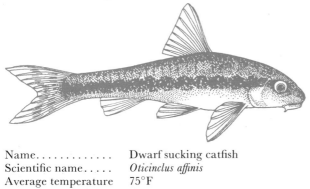

Name	Dwarf sucking catfish
Scientific name	*Oticinclus affinis*
Average temperature	75°F
Community	Yes
Breeding	—
Reproduction	Oviparous
Natural location	Rio de Janeiro, Brazil

Like all catfish, the dwarf sucking catfish is a scavenger, but with a difference—it has a sucking organ. This organ is really an extension of the lips,

Scatophagus argus

and a very useful piece of equipment it is, because it enables the fish to climb all over the plants, up one side and down the other, removing algæ as it travels. Although not a highly coloured fish, it has a charm in the streamlined shape of its body. The average length for an adult is 1¾ in. The body colouring is a darkish-brown, lightening as it approaches the underparts, and is overlaid with a slightly darker mottling.

Another peculiarity of this fish is that it will sometimes swim upside down immediately below the water surface, clinging to it as it apparently sucks in any floating food.

The sucking catfish is an interesting exhibit in any tank, quite inoffensive and fairly hardy. Unfortunately it is rarely bred in the aquarium.

Scats

The 'scats' belong to the sub-order Percoidei and are grouped under the family Scatophagidae. These fish have laterally compressed bodies and are found in brackish and salt water. The dorsal fin has spines on the fore part and soft rays on the rear part. Both parts of the dorsal fin are joined at the base. The anal fin is similar, with four or more spines at the front and soft rays at the rear.

Name	Spotted scat
Scientific name	*Scatophagus argus*
Average temperature	73°F
Community	No
Breeding	—
Reproduction	Oviparous
Natural location	East Indies

S. argus has a very slim, laterally compressed body, which is almost disc-like in outline. It is coloured grey to green, or pink to bronze-yellow, and is marked by large circular spots that vary in colour from a dark green to black. The body colour and markings are so variable with this species that they are often erroneously thought to be different species.

There are a number of sub-species, but as these have not as yet been accurately classified the aquarist can consider these various sub-species as *S. argus.*

Under natural conditions these fish are found in brackish water, and for this reason it has not been designated here as a community specimen. It can be kept in a fresh water aquarium, however, if a little salt is added to the water—one ounce of sea salt to eight gallons of water, or preferably one part of sea water to 20 parts of fresh water. If no salt is added, the water should be maintained in an alkaline condition of pH 7·4 or a little above. Brackish water is, however, preferable.

Although the spotted scats grow to 12-in. long in their natural environment, aquarium specimens rarely exceed 4 in. They are active, harmless fish, and become quite tame when acclimatised.

To date, they have not been bred in captivity, and no certain means have yet been determined to differentiate the sexes.

These fish are natural scavengers and are found in estuaries, mouths of rivers, and harbours of tropical ports. They are omnivorous and will eat almost anything.

Name............	— —
Scientific name.....	*Selenotoca papuensis*
Average temperature	73°F
Community.......	No (see below)
Breeding	—
Reproduction	Oviparous
Natural location....	New Guinea

This fish has a general body colour of silver marked with seven or eight black vertical bands on the upper part of the body; these bands break up into spots on the lower part of the body. The spiny dorsal and lips are black. The body shape is vertically compressed and oval, similar to *Scatophagus argus*. These fish have never been bred in captivity, and there is no known method of determining the sexes. Adult aquarium specimens attain a length of 4 in.

Although it is not considered a community fish, because it normally inhabits brackish water, *S. papuensis* can be acclimatised to fresh water if the transition is gradual. It can then be included in a community of fresh-water tropical fish, providing the other members are about the same size.

Marine tropicals

This small selection of fish suitable for marine aquaria has been restricted intentionally. It is true that experienced aquarists have successfully maintained sea-water tanks with a much larger selection, but it must be stressed that keeping marine tropicals is considerably more difficult than keeping fresh-water tropicals.

Natural foods are difficult, almost impossible, to obtain and we have to resort to near alternatives. The confines of the aquarium provide a very restricted volume of water when compared with the sea, and little is known about treatment of the fish should they become sick.

To experienced fresh-water aquarists, marine aquaria offer a challenging and exciting stage of progression, but to the novice it can prove an expensive and exasperating experience.

Of all the fish living naturally in salt water, very few will adapt themselves to the confines of the small aquarium in the home. The following short list is intended as an introduction to marine fish and offers suggestions of fish that can be kept satisfactorily in the home aquarium.

In general, the temperature suitable for these fish is between 70°F and 75°F.

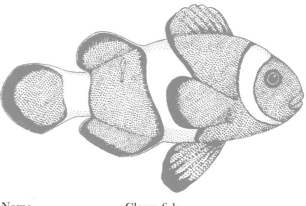

Name............	Clown fish
Scientific name.....	*Amphiprion percula*
Natural location....	Indian Ocean to Malay Archipelago

The clown fish has much to recommend it as a fish for the beginner. It is reasonably easy to obtain, it is not too large—about 2-in. long—it is very colourful, and most important it is hardy.

Clown fish are brilliantly and dramatically coloured a rich yellow, with three irregular white stripes—one near the eye, the second from the dorsal fin to the under-belly, and the third on the root of the tail. The design is further enhanced by thin, jet black lines edging the white stripes, and with black edgings to the yellow-brown fins.

In their natural habitat among the coral reefs they are very territorially minded—having selected a particular crevice they will guard it against intruders. In the aquarium they are lively and busy, but they are harmless.

Clown fish are partial to young guppies, brine shrimps, and also very fine pieces of raw fish. They have not yet been bred in an aquarium.

Other varieties suitable for marine aquaria include *A. ephiprion* and *A. sebae.*

Pomacentrus fuscus

Name. . . . .   Blue devil
Scientific name. . . . .   *Pomacentrus fuscus*
Natural location. . . .   Florida and West Indies

The blue devil is a sprightly, energetic fish that attains a length of about 4½ in. Its body colour is mainly dark grey to purple with rows of brilliant sapphire blue scales running along the body, and there are sprinkled high-lights of the same colour on the head. The tail and tips of the unpaired fins are yellow.

These fish are best kept singularly, but if other fish are included good refuges must be provided.

Name. . . . .   Black and white damsel fish
Scientific name. . . . .   *Dascyllus aruanus*
Natural location. . . .   East Indies to South Pacific Isles

The black and white damsel fish is another fish that has striking colour. The basic body colour is brilliant pearl white, with three vertical black bands—one through the eye, a second down the mid-body, and the third near the tail. The average size for adult fish is 2 in.

These fish are lively little fellows, but quarrel with their own species. It is advisable, therefore, to have only one specimen in the community tank.

Name. . . . .   White spotted fish
Scientific name. . . . .   *Dascyllus trimaculatus*
Natural location. . . .   Red Sea to East Indies

This fish has a black body and three brilliant white, enamel-like spots—one on the forehead, and one each side of the body just below the dorsal fin. The average size for adult fish is 2-in. long.

Its habits are similar to *D. aruanus* and it is advisable to limit the community to only one of these species, otherwise they will fight continually among themselves.

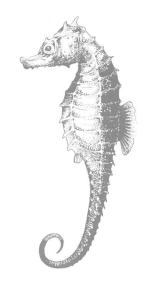

Name. . . . .   Sea horse
Scientific name. . . . .   *Hippocampus species*

The sea horse is not a particularly attractive fish for aquaria, in fact it is rather a grotesque creature with its long horse-like face and curled prehensile tail. Nevertheless, it is interesting if only for its unusual breeding habits.

During late spring, or early summer, the female deposits about a hundred eggs in a pouch situated on the belly of the male. They are then incubated for a period of about 40–50 days. The young then appear as free swimming individuals, still with remnants of the yolk sac.

Raising the youngsters is a real problem. They are slow moving little creatures that require live foods. Brine shrimps are best, but they can also be fed with small daphnia.

Sea horses vary in size depending upon species. The largest ones attain a length of about 12 in. They propel themselves by the dorsal fin, but like to anchor themselves to something with their prehensile tails, therefore it is necessary to provide branching coral, or some well weathered branches of trees for this purpose.

Name. . . . .   Velvet coral fish
Scientific name. . . . .   *Premnas biaculeatus*
Natural location. . . .   India, Malay Archipelago

The body colour is a rich brown marked with three yellow bands, the edges of which are tinged green. One of these bands is positioned across the centre of the body, another across the head, and the third across the tail root. The fins are all brown, or brownish, and edged with black.

Dascyllus trimaculatus

Index